GOVERNMENT
AND THE
ECONOMY

*Outstanding Studies
and Recent Dissertations*

Stuart Bruchey
University of Maine
General Editor

A Garland Series

The Efficacy
of Antidumping Duties

James M. DeVault

Garland Publishing, Inc.
New York & London
1993

Library of Congress Cataloging-in-Publication Data

DeVault, James M., 1961–
    The efficacy of antidumping duties / James M. DeVault.
        p.   cm. — (Government and the economy : outstanding studies and recent dissertations)
    A revision of the author's thesis (doctoral)—University of Wisconsin, 1990.
    Includes bibliographical references and index.
    ISBN 0–8153–1222–9 (alk. paper)
    1. Antidumping duties—United States. 2. Antidumping duties—Law and legislation—United States. I. Title. II. Series: Government and the economy.
HF1757.D48   1993
382'.73—dc20   92-2465
                                                          CIP

Printed on acid-free, 250-year-life paper
Manufactured in the United States of America

To My Mother

Contents

Tables

Preface

The postwar era has been characterized by unprecedented economic expansion. The rapid growth in international trade which occurred during this period contributed significantly to this expansion. The growth in international trade itself has been the product of several factors, but one of the most important was undoubtedly the multilateral trade liberalization brought about by the GATT. The GATT, which went into effect in 1947, reduced tariff barriers dramatically and established internationally accepted rules for the use of non-tariff barriers. Nonetheless, during the last two decades, protectionism has been on the rise. A major reason for this rise has been an increase in the use of non-tariff barriers. The purpose of this study is to explore how the use of one of these barriers, antidumping laws, has influenced the U.S. economy.

The work presented here represents a revised version of my doctoral dissertation, which was completed at the University of Wisconsin in 1990. My dissertation advisor, Robert E. Baldwin, has contributed to this work in many ways. Professor Baldwin originally suggested the topic to me and provided invaluable advice and encouragement throughout the process. I would also like to thank J. David Richardson. Professor Richardson's critical comments greatly improved my work and taught me much about the profession. Thanks are also due to Jim Walker, whose technical assistance was greatly appreciated. Most importantly, I would like to thank my family. I am particularly grateful to my wife Elizabeth, who sacrificed much along the way. Her patience, love, and understanding were a very important part of this project.

The Efficacy
of Antidumping Duties

Introduction

The phenomenon of dumping takes place in international trade when a firm sells a product abroad at a price which is beneath its fair value.[1] The international community, as represented by the GATT, views dumping as a form of unfair competition and gives governments the right to retaliate against foreign firms who engage in dumping. This retaliation takes the form of an antidumping duty, which is a discriminatory tariff levied only against the guilty firms' exports. The importance of antidumping duties has risen over the last decade as the number of dumping cases has steadily increased. Between 1980 and 1991, the United States alone conducted more than 500 antidumping investigations and imposed nearly 200 antidumping duties. Other restrictive measures were taken in many of the U.S. antidumping cases that did not produce duties.

Most economists would argue that dumping is beneficial if it promotes competition. This is because lower foreign prices raise the welfare of domestic consumers and also force domestic firms to produce more efficiently. From the economist's standpoint, dumping should be restricted only if it threatens to reduce domestic welfare. Such a reduction might occur if low foreign prices drive domestic firms out of business. This outcome is undesirable because foreign firms may then raise prices above their competitive level and thereby lower the welfare of domestic consumers. This outcome will occur, however, only if there are barriers to entry which prevent domestic firms or other foreign firms from re-entering the domestic market. It is only in this special situation that antidumping duties are justified in the eyes of most economists.[2]

The idea that this type of predatory dumping might reduce domestic welfare originally motivated Congress to pass the Antidumping Act of 1916, which first provided for antidumping

3

duties specifically targeted at predatory dumping. Subsequent laws, however, undermined the idea that only predatory dumping was a form of unfair competition. These laws defined as unfair any price discrimination in which the U.S. price of a foreign product was below the foreign price. These laws also prohibited foreign firms from charging prices which were beneath the average cost of production. There is little doubt now that the purpose of antidumping laws is to provide protection to domestic industries. If this were not the case, U.S. firms, who routinely engage in price discrimination as well as pricing below average cost, would be restricted from engaging in these "unfair" practices just as their foreign counterparts are.[3] Thus the U.S. antidumping laws serve primarily to provide protection to domestic industries. They do so by restricting (or threatening to restrict) the prices foreign firms can charge.

Since the U.S. antidumping laws serve mainly to protect domestic interests, how effective are these laws at providing relief? This is the question which I try to answer in this study. I answer this question in two parts. First, I examine how the U.S. antidumping laws are administered. The key question at this stage is what are the determinants of the protection provided by the U.S. antidumping laws? To answer this question, I first examine U.S. antidumping law and discuss the outcomes of the U.S. antidumping cases completed between 1980 and 1991. In so doing, I show that the U.S. antidumping laws provide relief to domestic industries through a number of different channels. Antidumping duties are only one of several forms of protection available; others include provisional duties, voluntary restraint agreements, and price or suspension agreements.

I then look at the institutional structure which determines whether industries receive relief and if so, how much. I examine first how antidumping duties are determined and then consider the conditions industries must meet to qualify for protection. I also explore the question of whether protection is administered objectively. This question has generated much research in recent years because U.S. antidumping institutions are designed to be insulated from political pressure. Several authors have shown that biases do exist, and I explore several issues which have not previously been considered.

In the second part of the book, I am concerned not with the administration of protection but rather with the efficacy of the protection provided. The main question I try to answer in this part is whether antidumping duties are an effective way of providing relief to domestic industries. To answer this question, I construct both theoretical and empirical models of antidumping duties. I then analyze the extent of the relief provided by antidumping duties. The theoretical model employs a three country monopolistically competitive framework to determine how much protection is provided and at what cost. The empirical model uses a non-linear least squares model to simulate the effects of two antidumping duties levied in the mid 1980s. This model is of interest because it allows for an arbitrary pattern of substitution between domestic output and imports from different countries.

In both models, I also explore the question of whether the protection provided by antidumping duties might be provided more effectively (in terms of reductions in national welfare) by an alternative trade policy. The alternative trade policy I consider is a non-discriminatory safeguard. A safeguard is a non-discriminatory trade impediment which is used to protect domestic industries from serious but not unfair import competition. A safeguard is used as a point of comparison for several reasons. First, it is the only alternative to antidumping duties which is consistent with the GATT. Second, antidumping duties have become a substitute for safeguards in the eyes of many international economists. This is a curious argument in that antidumping duties are discriminatory and hence are accompanied by trade diversion, which serves to undermine the protection they provide. Because safeguards are non-discriminatory, they are not accompanied by trade diversion and thus would appear to be more effective at providing relief to domestic industries. However, safeguards are often accompanied by legally sanctioned retaliation, something which is not overtly possible with antidumping duties. Furthermore, because the imported and domestic product may be differentiated, it is possible that the welfare effects of discriminatory and non-discriminatory trade policies might be reversed. This can occur if the imports penalized by the antidumping duty contribute less to domestic welfare than the imports penalized by the safeguard. Thus the question of which policy is more effective is open.

NOTES

1. Fair value can be defined in several different ways. The most frequently used definition of fair value is the price of the dumped product in the home market. See Chapter 2 for a more detailed discussion of fair value.

2. See Hindley [1991] for a thorough discussion of this point.

3. While both U.S. and foreign firms are restricted from engaging in predatory pricing, cases of predatory pricing, involving either domestic or foreign firms, are generally considered to be quite rare.

Part I: The Administration of Antidumping Duties

In the first part of the book, I examine the nature of the protection provided by the U.S. antidumping laws as well as the institutions responsible for providing it. The first chapter examines the outcomes of the 516 antidumping cases completed between 1980 and 1991. This chapter details the various outcomes and examines the countries and industries involved in antidumping cases. The second chapter examines the institutions responsible for administering the U.S. antidumping laws. The role played by these institutions is analyzed, as is the question of whether there is any bias in the decisions of these institutions.

Chapter 1: U.S.
Antidumping Actions and
Outcomes

1.1 Introduction

In this chapter, I provide an overview of how U.S. antidumping law is administered. The purpose of the chapter is to describe how the law works (both in theory and in practice) and who has been affected by it. I begin by briefly describing U.S. antidumping law. Next, I examine the outcomes of all the antidumping cases filed between 1980 and 1991. These outcomes are then broken done according to the countries and industries involved. Finally, I examine the large number of antidumping cases which were withdrawn during this time period. These cases are of interest because several authors have argued that most of them were withdrawn only after the domestic industries involved reached collusive agreements with foreign firms which were detrimental to domestic welfare.

1.2 A Summary of U.S. Antidumping Law

Current U.S. antidumping laws are contained in the Trade Agreements Act of 1979 and its subsequent revisions in 1984 and 1988. An antidumping investigation is typically initiated when a domestic firm (or group of firms) presents a petition to the two agencies who administer the U.S. antidumping laws: the International Trade Administration (ITA) and the International Trade Commission (ITC).[1] This petition provides information on the nature of the dumping as well as the foreign firms involved.

If the ITA finds that the petition contains sufficient information, an antidumping investigation is initiated.

Two conditions must be met before an antidumping duty is imposed: first, dumping must be shown to exist; second, dumping must be shown to be the cause of "material injury" to a domestic industry. The ITA is responsible for determining whether dumping exists while the ITC is responsible for determining whether material injury has resulted from the dumping.

In each antidumping case, each agency may make both a preliminary and a final ruling. Within 45 days of the filing of the petition, the ITC must make its preliminary decision. If it finds no reasonable indication of material injury, the case is dismissed. If there is a reasonable indication of material injury, the investigation will continue.

Given an affirmative preliminary decision by the ITC, the ITA then has 160 days from the filing of the petition to reach its preliminary decision.[2] Unlike the ITC's preliminary decision, however, a negative preliminary ruling by the ITA will not lead to a dismissal of the case. The preliminary decision of the ITA is still important, however, because an affirmative decision produces provisional relief for the domestic industry. This relief takes two forms: first, the liquidation of the dumped imports is suspended; second, a bond equivalent to the estimated value of the antidumping penalties must be posted by any importer of the dumped goods.[3]

Once the ITA has reached its preliminary decision, it then has 75 days to make its final determination.[4] If this determination is negative, the case is dismissed and any provisional relief is revoked. If the ITA's final determination is positive, the ITC then has to make its final determination within 45 days of the ITA's final determination or within 120 days of the ITA's preliminary determination, whichever is later.[5] A negative final decision by the ITC leads to the dismissal of the petition and the revoking of any provisional measures. An affirmative final decision by the ITC leads to the issuing of an antidumping order by the ITA. This order is issued to U.S Customs and specifies the rate at which the antidumping duty is levied as well as the imports against which it is levied.

Antidumping investigations are terminated or suspended prematurely in several situations. Antidumping investigations are terminated prematurely when the antidumping petition is withdrawn. Petitioners may withdraw a petition if they feel the likelihood of obtaining relief is small or if the legal costs involved in continuing the case are too great. Petitions may also be withdrawn if domestic and foreign firms (or their governments) can reach an agreement which mitigates the effects of the dumping. Suspension of an antidumping investigation occurs when foreign firms agree to eliminate the injurious effects of the dumping. This agreement usually involves a pledge by foreign firms to either raise prices or to cease exporting the dumped merchandise. The antidumping investigation will remain suspended as long as the foreign firms keep their promise.

Any agreement (suspension or otherwise) reached after the ITA has initiated its investigation must be found by the ITA to be in the public interest. This means that the agreement must involve a smaller welfare loss than that which would occur under an antidumping duty. Unfortunately, the law does not specify how welfare is calculated and thus it is unclear how the public interest enters into the ITA's decision to accept or reject an agreement.[6] If the ITA has not initiated an investigation when an agreement is reached, it cannot restrict the agreement in this way.

In summary, antidumping duties are levied only when the preliminary decision of the ITC and the final decisions of the ITA and ITC are affirmative. Even when one of these decisions is negative, domestic firms may still receive some relief through provisional measures. Domestic firms may also obtain relief if they can reach an agreement with the foreign firms responsible for the dumping.

1.3 U.S. Antidumping Outcomes

Having discussed the current U.S. antidumping laws, I now examine the outcomes of the 516 antidumping cases completed between 1980 and 1991. These cases were selected for study because they were all filed under the Trade Agreements Act of 1979, which substantially altered previous U.S. antidumping law. I then examine the preliminary and final decisions of the ITA and ITC. These decisions are important because they determine how much provisional relief is provided. Next, I consider the pattern of outcomes according to the countries and industries involved. I conclude by examining the cases which were withdrawn prior to their completion.

1.3.1 The Overall Pattern of Outcomes

Table 1-1 breaks down the outcomes of the 516 antidumping cases completed between 1980 and 1991. The table also lists these outcomes by the year in which they were reached. Table 1-1 reveals that the U.S. antidumping laws produce antidumping duties in about 37% of all cases. This does not mean, however, that relief was not provided in the remaining cases. As we will see shortly, provisional protection was provided in many of the negative outcomes. Furthermore, 23% of all antidumping cases were terminated prematurely because the petitions supporting them were withdrawn. Whether or not these petitions were withdrawn as a result of collusive agreements between domestic and foreign firms is unclear from Table 1-1. I show later, however, that a large majority of these petitions were withdrawn after restrictive agreements had been reached between U.S. and foreign steelmakers.

When the outcomes are considered year by year, it is apparent that there is no obvious trend toward affirmative or negative outcomes. The pattern of outcomes does not appear to be more protectionist in recent years and, if anything, has become less protectionist. The year by year outcomes also show that there has been a steep reduction in the number of cases withdrawn since 1986. While 23% of all cases were withdrawn over the entire 11 year period, only about 6% of the cases completed between 1987 and 1991 were withdrawn. The reason for this trend is that most of the withdrawn cases were withdrawn after comprehensive voluntary restraint agreements had been reached with foreign steel makers in the early and mid-1980s. Once these agreements had been reached, the U.S. steel industry ceased filing dumping petitions for the most part.

Table 1-1: Antidumping outcomes according to the year in which
            they were reached

Year	Affirmative	Negative	Withdrawn	Total
1980	6	16	9	31
1981	3	6	4	13
1982	5	20	24	49
1983	13	17	4	34
1984	20	19	11	50
1985	11	25	42	78
1986	29	22	13	64
1987	39	14	2	55
1988	8	6	1	15
1989	24	21	2	47
1990	13	8	3	24
1991	19	34	3	56
Total	190	208	118	516
As % of total outcomes	37	40	23	100

Source: Author's compilation based on data from the *Federal
Register.*

1.3.2 The Extent of Provisional Protection

In this section, I examine the pattern of the antidumping decisions reached by the ITA and the ITC. I also examine the extent of the provisional relief received by domestic industries between 1980 and 1991. Table 1-2 provides data on the preliminary and final decisions reached by the ITA and the ITC during the years 1980 through 1991. Consider first the preliminary decision of the ITC, which is important because a negative determination leads to the dismissal of the case. Table 1-2 shows that about 22% of the cases which required a preliminary decision by the ITC were rejected. Since the most frivolous cases do not require a preliminary decision by the ITC, the cases rejected by the ITC at this juncture are based on something more than mere allegations. But how much of an indication of injury is necessary before the ITC will rule in the affirmative?

While the exact injury threshold varies from case to case, it seems likely that the preliminary decision of the ITC will be biased in favor of the domestic industry. Because the ITC has only 45 days to make its preliminary decision, there is only a limited amount of evidence available to it, much of which is unsubstantiated. In many cases, the absence of data from other sources leads to an over-reliance by the ITC on the data contained in the petition, which has usually been carefully prepared by the petitioners to support their case. Thus it is likely that the preliminary decision of the ITC is biased in favor of the domestic industry.

Looking at the pattern of preliminary ITC decisions over the observation period, there is a trend in recent years toward more affirmative decisions. For example, between 1980 and 1985, roughly 76% of the cases were preliminarily affirmed; between 1986 and 1991, roughly 81% of the cases were affirmed. Moreover, between 1987 and 1990, 89% of the cases were affirmed. This tendency to preliminary affirm most cases, especially in recent years, has had unfortunate consequences for the foreign firms involved, as we shall see shortly.

Consider next the ITA's preliminary decision. Table 1-2 indicates that this decision is negative in about 6% of the cases

Table 1-2: Preliminary and final decisions of the ITA and the ITC
(A - affirmative, N - negative)

	Preliminary decisions				Final decisions			
	ITC		ITA		ITA		ITC	
	A	N	A	N	A	N	A	N
1980	18	12	10	1	10	1	6	3
1981	7	3	5	2	4	2	3	1
1982	29	19	24	2	6	0	5	1
1983	23	7	21	2	20	3	13	7
1984	46	4	33	7	30	6	20	9
1985	61	13	47	4	27	5	11	7
1986	47	11	45	2	40	2	30	9
1987	52	2	51	1	48	3	39	9
1988	13	2	13	0	11	1	8	3
1989	40	5	38	2	38	2	23	14
1990	17	6	16	0	16	0	14	2
1991	32	22	31	0	31	0	19	12
Total	385	106	334	23	281	25	191	77

Source: Author's compilation based on data from the *Federal Register* and the *Operation of the Trade Agreements Program*

which come before it, a number which is quite low. There are three explanations for why this figure is so low. First, many of the weaker cases have been previously eliminated, increasing the probability of an affirmative decision. Second, cases are normally rejected only if the dumping margin is less than one half of one percent. Third, the procedures used by the ITA to compute dumping margins have an upward bias. Murray [1991] and others have shown that several significant biases do exist and that these biases favor the domestic industry. Whether or not the 7% rejection rate is low, the large number of affirmative preliminary decisions made by the ITA produces provisional protection in roughly 66% of all antidumping cases. Thus although only 37% of the antidumping cases eventually produce antidumping duties, some measure of relief is obtained in at least 66% of all cases.

Consider next the final determination of the ITA. Table 1-2 shows that this determination is negative in about 8% of the cases which come before the ITA. Thus only a few cases are dismissed as a result of the ITA's final decision. This is particularly true in recent years. Between 1986 and 1991, only 3% of the ITA's final decisions were negative. In 1990 and 1991, the ITA made no negative final determinations.

Finally, consider the ITC's final determination. Table 1-2 indicates that this determination is negative in about 29% of the cases, a figure which appears reasonable given the screening process involved. This figure should dispel any notion that the ITC's final injury determination is automatic. Nonetheless, the figure is disturbing in that it suggests a considerable misuse of provisional antidumping measures. The data in Table 1-2 shows that provisional measures were taken in 77 cases against foreign firms whose dumping was innocuous. This represents about 15% of all the antidumping cases filed between 1980 and 1991.

Ideally, any negative determinations made by the ITC should come at the preliminary stage of the investigation. In fact, of the cases which required a final decision by the ITC, almost 30% involved a reversal of the ITC's preliminary affirmative decision. This suggests that the ITC has insufficient time in which to make its preliminary determination. This has negative consequences not only for the foreign firms unjustly punished by the provisional measures, but also for the domestic firms who must invest a considerable amount of time and money during the investigation, and for the public, which must bear the cost of both the ITA's and ITC's investigations, a cost which is far from negligible. One simple way to reduce the likelihood of a reversal by the ITC is to provide the ITC with more time in which to make its preliminary decision.

Having considered the question of provisional protection, I now turn to a frequency analysis of the countries and industries involved in antidumping investigations.

1.3.3 Country by Country Antidumping Outcomes

Table 1-3 provides data on the number of antidumping cases filed against various nations between 1980 and 1991. Table 1-3 also breaks down the outcomes for each country and gives the average dumping margin levied against imports from each country (when no duties have been levied against a country, the average dumping margin is set equal to zero.) Notice first that the mean overall antidumping duty is 38.2%. This is nearly 8 times as great as the average U.S. MFN tariff rate on dutiable imports for this period and is some 65% greater than the equivalent antidumping duty rate reported by Messerlin [1988] for the EC.

Turning to the results for individual countries, Japan is the country which is most heavily penalized by U.S. antidumping duties. Japanese firms are involved in 12% of the antidumping investigations and are the target of 21% of the antidumping duties levied. In addition, the average antidumping duty levied against Japanese firms is close to 61%, a rate which exceeds the overall average by 60%. Other countries which are heavily penalized include Brazil, China, Taiwan, and Germany.

The developed countries and the Asian NICs are involved in about 70% of the antidumping investigations and 66% of the withdrawals. They are the target of 68% of the duties levied. The severity of the duties levied against the developed countries and the NICs, however, is lower than one might expect. With the exception of Japan and a few other nations, the average antidumping duties for these countries are low. Countries such

Table 1-3: Country by country summary of U.S. antidumping outcomes, 1980-1991 (W - withdrawal, N - negative, A - affirmative)

	Cases filed	Outcomes W	Outcomes N	Outcomes A	Mean duty
Overall	516	118	208	190	38.2
DCs	288	71	123	94	41.3
Australia	3	1	2	0	0.0
Austria	7	1	6	0	0.0
Belgium	11	5	5	1	14.7
Canada	27	3	14	10	13.2
Finland	5	4	1	0	0.0
France	23	7	10	6	22.6
Germany	41	14	16	11	29.3
Greece	2	0	1	1	36.7
Ireland	1	0	1	0	0.0
Italy	27	3	15	9	39.2
Japan	64	7	18	39	60.9
Luxembourg	6	2	4	0	0.0
Netherlands	10	4	5	1	17.0
New Zealand	2	0	1	1	26.9
Norway	2	0	1	1	23.8
Portugal	3	2	1	0	0.0
Spain	15	8	4	3	38.8
Sweden	7	0	2	5	43.1
Switzerland	4	1	3	0	0.0
United Kingdom	23	8	11	4	25.3
Asian NICs	75	7	33	35	19.4
Hong Kong	4	0	2	2	4.8
Singapore	8	0	4	4	18.7
South Korea	29	2	12	15	14.6
Taiwan	34	4	16	14	26.8

Table 1-3: (continued)

	Cases filed	Outcomes W	Outcomes N	Outcomes A	Mean duty
LDCs	153	41	51	61	44.1
Argentina	9	0	5	4	63.3
Brazil	27	6	10	11	39.9
Chile	3	0	1	2	28.8
China	27	1	7	19	50.1
Columbia	4	1	2	1	3.5
Costa Rica	1	0	0	1	0.7
Czechoslovakia	2	2	0	0	0.0
Ecuador	1	0	0	1	5.9
El Salvador	1	0	1	0	0.0
Hungary	5	3	1	1	7.4
India	4	0	2	2	4.0
Iran	1	0	0	1	241.1
Israel	5	1	2	2	6.9
Kenya	1	0	0	1	1.6
Malaysia	1	0	1	0	0.0
Mexico	10	2	5	3	35.3
Peru	1	0	1	0	0.0
Philippines	1	0	1	0	0.0
Poland	7	5	2	0	0.0
Romania	9	5	1	3	52.1
South Africa	7	6	0	1	3.3
Thailand	4	0	1	3	12.1
Trinidad	1	0	0	1	9.8
Turkey	4	1	2	1	33.0
USSR	2	0	1	1	64.9
Venezuela	13	7	4	2	132.5
Yugoslavia	7	2	3	2	22.2

Source: Author's compilation based on data from the *Federal Register* and the *Operation of the Trade Agreements Program*.

as Canada, France, and South Korea have fared quite well in this regard.

The developing countries, except for Brazil and China, do not appear to be penalized severely by antidumping duties. The LDCs and China account for 32% of the duties levied, but when Brazil and China are excluded, this figure drops to 16%. While the average antidumping duty rates for the developing countries are quite high at 44%, this average is inflated considerably by the duties levied against Argentina, Brazil, China, Iran, and Venezuela. For the remaining developing countries, the average margin is only about 21%.

1.3.3 Industry by Industry Antidumping Outcomes

Table 1-4 provides a summary of U.S. antidumping outcomes according to industry SIC groupings for the years 1980-1991. For each industry, the outcome of each case is provided along with the average antidumping duty levied (where no duties have been levied, the average rate is set equal to zero.)

The industry group which has made the most intense use of U.S. antidumping law is primary and fabricated metal products. This industry group alone accounts for over 45% of the petitions filed, over 40% of the duties levied, and over 80% of the withdrawn cases. A significant majority of the cases in this industry group involve steel products. In assessing the extent of the relief provided to this industry group, two things are important. First, many of the cases filed were eventually withdrawn. I discuss this issue in greater detail in the next section, but most of these withdrawals were the result of quantitative agreements involving the U.S. steel industry. Thus some relief was obtained in these cases. Second, while a large number of duties were levied, the mean rates of these duties were 25% below the overall average.

Industries such as chemicals, textiles and electric and non-electric equipment have also successfully used the antidumping laws to obtain relief. These industries have been successful in several ways. First, many duties have been levied against their

Table 1-4: Industry by industry summary of U.S. antidumping outcomes, 1980-91 (W - withdrawal, N - negative, A - affirmative)

	Cases filed	Outcomes W	Outcomes N	Outcomes A	Mean duty
Overall	516	118	208	190	34.8
Agriculture	19	1	7	11	31.7
Food prod.	9	0	7	2	11.0
Textiles	24	2	11	11	41.9
Apparel	2	0	2	0	0.0
Furniture	4	1	3	0	0.0
Paper prod.	10	0	10	0	0.0
Printing	3	1	0	2	34.3
Chemicals	77	8	30	39	53.8
Oil prod.	1	0	0	1	6.6
Rubber prod.	6	1	5	0	0.0
Mineral prod.	25	0	23	2	61.6
Metal prod.	241	97	67	77	26.9
Non-electric eq.	48	2	24	22	43.2
Electric eq.	30	4	9	17	39.5
Transport eq.	7	1	5	1	3.7
Miscellaneous	10	0	5	5	64.4

Source: Author's compilation based on data from the *Federal Register* and the *Operation of the Trade Agreements Program*.

foreign competitors. Second, the mean duty rates in these cases have been high. Finally, many of the cases which have not produced relief have been withdrawn, raising the possibility that these cases were withdrawn after restrictive agreements had been reached.

Finally, the concentration of antidumping duties across industry groups is remarkable. The five industry groups mentioned above (chemicals, metals, textiles and electric and non-electric equipment) account for 81% of the cases filed, 96% of the cases withdrawn, and 87% of the duties levied. This concentration is probably a reflection of the international competition which exists in these industries. The concentration of cases in these industries also reflects the experience and knowledge which is gained through repeated exposure to the antidumping process. This is certainly the case in the steel industry, which has made the most extensive use of the U.S. antidumping laws.

1.3.4 Withdrawals

The large number of cases withdrawn between 1980 and 1991 is an interesting feature of Table 1-1. As was mentioned earlier, one reason a case might be withdrawn is that the domestic or foreign firms involved (or their governments) reach an agreement which mitigates the effect of the alleged dumping. These agreements may take several forms, including quantitative restrictions or suspension agreements (i.e. price agreements), but they all involve negotiations between domestic and foreign firms or their governments.

Both Prusa [1988, 1990] and Staiger and Wolak [1989] have argued that such negotiations allow for collusive agreements which are detrimental to domestic welfare. Prusa in particular argues that the U.S. antidumping laws are misused by domestic firms seeking to reach collusive agreements. He claims that large industries can get relief by filing multiple antidumping petitions simultaneously. The threat that these petitions will produce antidumping duties (and an international trade dispute) in turn leads to negotiated settlements and withdrawal of the antidumping cases. Whether or not the antidumping cases have merit is irrelevant; it is the threat that counts. If this is true, then the number of duties levied will seriously understate the amount of protection provided by the antidumping laws.[7]

To address the question of misuse, the cases involving withdrawn petitions are now carefully reviewed. Table 1-5 provides a summary of the motives specified in the *Federal Register* for the withdrawal of cases. Table 1-5 shows that 76 cases were withdrawn as a result of three agreements involving the U.S. steel industry and its foreign competitors. I will consider these cases separately in a moment. Of the 42 remaining withdrawn petitions, 4 involved inadequate petitions while 8 involved petitions which were withdrawn, amended, and refiled. Suspension agreements were reached in 8 of the remaining cases and 1 case produced a VRA. The exact motive for withdrawal was unclear in the remaining 21 cases, but it seems likely that in several of these cases, withdrawal occurred because the chance of obtaining significant relief had dwindled.

The results of this review indicate that the large number of withdrawn cases is due primarily to the steel arrangements reached in 1980, 1982, and 1984. This is consistent with Prusa's argument that large industries filing multiple petitions receive protection via negotiated settlements. But the key to Prusa's argument is not that the antidumping laws lead to negotiated settlements but rather that these negotiated settlements result in unwarranted protection (if dumping is taking place and if it is causing material injury to a domestic industry, negotiated settlements should produce a smaller welfare loss for domestic consumers because these agreements must be found to be in the public interest.) Thus Prusa's argument will only hold if the protection provided by the steel arrangements would not have been obtained if the withdrawn cases had been completed. I now turn to an analysis of these arrangements.

The first arrangement took place in October of 1980, when 7 antidumping petitions were withdrawn by U.S. Steel in response to the strengthening of the Trigger Price Mechanism (TPM) by the U.S. Commerce Department. The withdrawn cases originally alleged that imports from the EC's major steel producers were being dumped in the U.S. In response to the filings, EC Commissioner Etienne Davignon threatened a trade war if the investigations continued. This put Commerce between

Table 1-5: Motives for withdrawing antidumping cases

Motive for withdrawal	Number of cases withdrawn	ITC case number (731-TA-
Steel Arrangements		
1980 TPM Revision	7	18-24
1982 EC Arrangement	20	53, 59-63, 65, 67, 69, 70, 72, 74, 82-86, 104-106
1984 Steel Import Program	49	158, 169-74, 176-83, 192-4, 197-8, 205, 209-10, 212-8, 220-3, 225-9, 235, 249-51, 256-8, 267-8, 274
Subtotal	76	
Other motives for withdrawal		
Inadequate petition	4	39, 43, 146, 515
Amend petition	8	34, 51, 97-99, 301-3
Suspension or price agreement reached	8	38, 45, 52, 58, 286, 288, 300, 374
VRA	1	118
Unknown	21	4, 66, 143, 147, 186, 190, 242, 253, 281, 306-7, 336, 350, 372, 436-8, 456, 463, 495-6
Subtotal	42	
Total withdrawals	118	

Source: Based on data from the *Federal Register*.

a rock and a hard place: on the one hand, there was ample evidence that dumping was taking place; on the other hand, if the investigations were consummated, the result would be a trade war.[8] The Commerce department responded to the crisis by strengthening the TPM. Because no duties or quantitative restrictions were applied, the trade war was averted. Because Commerce strengthened the TPM, this made it less likely that dumping would be a problem in the future. U.S. Steel was not overly satisfied with the new TPM, but eventually succumbed to government pressure and withdrew its antidumping petitions. According to Levine,

> Considerable government pressure was placed on US Steel (including members of the board) to withdraw its antidumping petitions, even though some or all of the cases would probably have resulted in positive findings.[9]

In this case, dumping was clearly taking place and hence the rather limited protection that was provided was not unwarranted.

The second steel agreement took place in 1982, when 20 cases were withdrawn after the U.S. and the European Community reached an agreement which established quantitative restrictions on the Community's steel exports to the U.S. The agreement was reached in response to the filing of a large number of antidumping and countervailing duty petitions by U.S. steel producers. The agreement was motivated by a desire on the part of the EC to avoid the imposition of antidumping and countervailing duties. These duties would almost certainly have been imposed because the ITA had found clear evidence of both dumping and subsidization. Howell et al state that

> The real implication ... was that if the U.S. trade laws were applied to the facts of the situation, a number of European firms would be excluded from the U.S. market entirely.[10]

Again, the antidumping laws were not being used to obtain relief which was unwarranted. In fact, the withdrawal of the antidumping and countervailing duty cases probably produced a smaller welfare loss for U.S. consumers because imposition of the antidumping and countervailing duties would have reduced the steel exports of several EC members by more than the agreement did.

The final agreement took place in 1984 when President Reagan signed into law the Steel Import Program (SIP). This program eventually resulted in the withdrawal of 49 antidumping petitions. The SIP arose out of a Section 201 case in which the ITC recommended the imposition of quantitative restrictions on several imported steel products. The President rejected this recommendation, but gave the U.S. Trade Representative the authority to negotiate voluntary restraint agreements (VRAs) with countries who engaged in unfair trade practices (excluding the EC which was already bound by the 1982 agreement.) In exchange for the VRAs, U.S. steel producers agreed to withdraw the antidumping and countervailing duty petitions which they had filed against the country. There is no doubt that these petitions were in some part responsible for the VRAs but there is ample evidence that dumping and subsidization were taking place on a wide scale. In describing this evidence, Howell et al [1988] note that

> The cumulative evidentiary effect of these dozens of cases -- each of which involved a detailed investigation by the U.S. government -- was to demonstrate that in the early and mid- 1980s, the U.S. was experiencing a wave of dumped and subsidized imports from virtually all points on the compass.[11]

Again, while the antidumping cases were in part responsible for the VRAs, it is also clear that dumping was taking place on a wide scale so that some relief was warranted.

Thus Prusa's argument that the antidumping laws are being used to obtain unwarranted protection via negotiated settlements does not appear to be valid. In most of the withdrawn cases, there is a substantial amount of evidence that dumping was taking place so that some measure of relief would have been obtained if the cases had not been withdrawn. Furthermore, if we look at the number of cases withdrawn in the last 5 years, we find that only about 5% of all the cases filed during this period were withdrawn. This suggests that allowing firms to withdraw petitions does not produce a greater degree of protection.

1.3.5 Summary

The results of this section can be summarized as follows. First, 190 antidumping duties have been imposed over the last 12 years, with an increasing number of these duties being imposed in recent years. This large number is not necessarily an indication that the administrative process is biased in favor of the domestic petitioner, however. During the same period, 208 antidumping investigations produced negative outcomes for domestic petitioners. Furthermore, the number of affirmative and negative outcomes has remained roughly balanced even in recent years. Second, even though only about one third of all antidumping cases result in the imposition of antidumping duties, provisional protection is provided in nearly two thirds of all antidumping cases. Third, protection was also provided in most of the withdrawn cases. But the large number of withdrawn cases is apparently not an indication that the U.S. antidumping laws are being misused by domestic firms seeking to obtain unwarranted protection. In the majority of the cases, evidence of dumping was present and hence some form of relief would have been obtained even if the cases had not been withdrawn. Indeed, it could be argued that by allowing cases to be withdrawn, the welfare loss in many of these cases was reduced.

Finally, the majority of antidumping cases are directed against exports from a small number of countries and industries. Brazil, China, Japan, and several European nations are the targets of most antidumping cases. With a couple of exceptions, developing countries do not appear to be adversely affected by U.S. antidumping laws. The industries which are most frequently involved in antidumping cases include primary and fabricated metals, electric and non-electric equipment, textiles, and chemicals. These industries are responsible for the vast majority of the cases filed and receive the majority of the relief provided.

NOTES

1. While domestic firms file most antidumping petitions, other domestic parties with sufficient standing (such as unions) may also file antidumping petitions. Antidumping petitions can also be filed by the ITA itself.

2. In cases deemed to be extraordinarily complicated, this deadline may be extended to 210 days.

3. If the liquidation of imports is suspended by U.S. Customs, the processing of the paperwork on these imports is suspended. The imports may still be bought and sold in the U.S., but by suspending the liquidation of these imports, Customs reserves the right to adjust the final duty.

4. This period may be extended to 135 days at the request of the exporter if the ITA's preliminary decision is affirmative or at the request of the petitioner if the ITA's preliminary decision is negative.

5. If the ITA's preliminary decision is negative, the ITC then has 75 days from the date of the ITA's final affirmative determination to make its final decision.

6. The law does list several factors which the ITA must take into account when evaluating how an agreement affects the public interest. These include the relative effects of the antidumping duty and the quantitative agreement on consumers, the domestic industry, and the international competitiveness of the U.S. economy. The law does not state how these various interests are to be weighed, however.

7. It has also been argued that the mere presence of an antidumping mechanism is likely to produce relief for domestic firms because it discourages foreign firms from pricing too aggressively. Herander and Schwartz [1984] find evidence which supports this argument.

8. See Howell et al, pg 521, and Levine, pg 15.

9. Levine [1985], pg 15.

10. Howell et al [1988], pg. 525.

11. Howell et al [1988], pg 527.

Chapter 2: Institutional Structure and Antidumping Policy

2.1 Introduction

U.S. trade policy over the last two decades has become increasingly reliant upon administered protection. As a result, the agencies responsible for administering protection in the U.S. (the International Trade Administration [ITA] and the International Trade Commission [ITC]) have become increasingly important. These agencies administer the U.S. unfair trade laws and their influence extends beyond these laws into other areas, such as escape clause actions.

Because the U.S. unfair trade laws have become the preferred route for many industries seeking protection, the role of the ITA and the ITC in administering these laws has come under considerable scrutiny. The main question has been whether or not these agencies have objectively administered the U.S. trade laws. In this chapter, I examine how the ITA and the ITC have implemented the U.S. antidumping laws. The goal is to determine whether the ITA and the ITC administer the U.S. antidumping laws in a consistent and impartial manner. This is an important question because any bias in the administration of the U.S. unfair trade laws is likely to increase the probability that protection is provided to domestic industries.

I begin the chapter by focusing on the role of the ITA. The ITA's role in antidumping cases is to determine whether dumping is taking place, and if so, to what extent. Other authors have examined the role of the ITA, including Murray [1991], Baldwin and Moore [1991], and Caine [1981]. I add to the analysis performed by these authors by examining in detail the dumping margins computed by the ITA between 1980 and 1991. I find that

29

the average dumping margin has been both large and increasing during this period. The reason for both trends is an increase in the use of one method of computing dumping margins. This method punishes certain foreign firms who do not or cannot comply fully with ITA investigators. This method punishes foreign firms unjustly in many cases.

After examining the role of the ITA, I then focus on the role played by the ITC in the administration of U.S. antidumping laws. The job of the ITC in antidumping investigations is to determine whether the dumped imports have materially injured a domestic industry or threaten to do so. Many other authors have examined the importance of economic criteria in the decisions made by the ITC. The results of Baldwin [1985] provide support for the hypothesis that the ITC has used economic criteria appropriately. But Baldwin examines only escape clause decisions, which represent a small fraction of total ITC decisions. Moore [1990] and Baldwin and Steagall [1991] also find some support for the argument that the ITC uses economic criteria in reaching its decisions, but both also find that political or political economic factors exert significant influence. Hansen [1990] finds that economic criteria are essentially irrelevant and that political factors motivate most ITC decisions. Prusa [1990] also finds little support for the argument that economic factors influence ITC decisions.

In summary, the available evidence suggests that economic criteria have a limited influence on ITC decisions. I attempt to clarify the role of economic criteria in ITC decisions by carefully modelling the way in which the ITC uses the economic criteria specified in the antidumping and countervailing duty laws. The novelty of this approach lies in the attention given to the procedures used by the ITC to evaluate the economic criteria. Previous studies have ignored questions related to the ITC's decision making process, and as a result, they have not fully identified the role of economic criteria in this process.

My results show that economic criteria play an important role in ITC decisions. While I do not control for political factors, the strong significance of the economic criteria suggests that ITC decisions are at least based loosely on the legally specified criteria. ITC decisions clearly are not motivated solely by political criteria.

I now begin my analysis of the roles of the ITA and the ITC in the administration of U.S. antidumping laws by examining the way in which the ITA computes dumping margins.

2.2 The ITA and Dumping Margins

A dumping margin represents the difference between the home or fair value of an imported product and its actual U.S. price. In this section, I analyze the methodologies used by the ITA to compute dumping margins between 1980 and 1991. The analysis has two objectives. The first objective is to determine the frequency with which the ITA has used different methodologies to compute dumping margins. The second objective is to determine whether some of these methodologies are more likely to produce protectionist outcomes.

2.2.1 The Computation of Dumping Margins in Theory

Before proceeding further, I provide a brief description of how the ITA computes dumping margins. At first glance, the ITA's task appears simple: it need only determine the exporter's home and U.S. market values, and then compare the two. If the former exceeds the latter, dumping is taking place. The dumping margin is then obtained by taking the percentage difference between the two market values.

In fact, the ITA's job is immensely complicated and involves considerable discretion on its part. The main reason for this is that there are many ways to compute the exporter's home and U.S. market values. To add to this problem, differences across countries in the product, in its circumstances of sale and in a myriad of other factors all serve to complicate matters further. All of these differences must be accounted for, and this requires that the exporter's home and U.S. market values be adjusted accordingly.

Consider first how the ITA determines the exporter's home market value. The ITA has five separate options for computing home market value. By law, if the foreign firm has adequate sales in its home market above the cost of production, home market value must be based on the firm's home price. If this is not the case, the ITA may use either the price of the product to a third country or the product's constructed value as a measure of home market value.[1] A constructed value represents the ITA's estimate of the foreign firm's production costs, including overhead and a margin for profit. If there is insufficient information to compute either a third country price or a constructed value, the ITA relies on the best information available, which can come from several sources, but is most often taken from the antidumping petition filed by the domestic industry. Data provided by the petitioner is frequently used to punish uncooperative foreign firms, or foreign firms who do not provide "timely" responses or who provide responses which are either inconsistent or impossible to verify. Finally, if the economy of the exporter is state-controlled, the ITA uses the following special procedure to determine home market value. First, if a surrogate price for the product is available from an appropriate market economy, that price is used. If such a price is not available, a constructed value is created based on the exporter's factors of production and the cost of these factors in an appropriate market economy.

Having discussed how the ITA determines the foreign firm's home market value, consider next how it determines the firm's U.S. market value. The ITA has three options here: the purchase price (PP), the exporter's sales price (ESP) or the best information available. The PP represents the price at which the exporter sells the product to an unrelated purchaser in the U.S. prior to the date of importation. If sales are made to a related party in the U.S. on or after the date of importation, the ESP is used. The ESP represents the price at which merchandise is sold by or for the account of the exporter. The major reason for the distinction between PP and ESP is that sales to a related party are suspect. If neither the PP or the ESP are available, the best information available is used.

Once the appropriate home and U.S. market values have been determined, they are then adjusted to account for any differences in the product, in its circumstances of sale or in any of a number of other factors. Determining what adjustments to both prices are necessary is one of the most complicated parts of the ITA's task. In many areas, the law is ambiguous, and this leaves ample room for discretion. Unfortunately, the sheer number and variety of adjustments makes it difficult to analyze the process in detail.

After having made all the necessary adjustments to the respective prices, the ITA must then compute the dumping margin. Since the ITA normally examines the home and U.S. prices of the dumped imports over a six month period, it must find some way of comparing these two different sets of prices. The standard procedure used by the ITA has been to average foreign prices over the six month period and then compare the average foreign price with the price at which each U.S. sale is made. When the average foreign price exceeds the U.S. price for a particular sale, the dumping margin for that sale is computed. When the reverse is true, the sale is disregarded. The final dumping margin is obtained by taking a weighted average of the individual dumping margins.

This process is clearly biased and virtually guarantees that some dumping will be found even when the foreign firm charges identical prices in both markets. The only time dumping will not be found is when the foreign firm charges roughly the same price in both markets over the entire six month period, something which is very unlikely. Since 1984, the ITA has been authorized to average both foreign and U.S. prices before making any price comparisons, something which would end this bias. It has rarely chosen to do so, however. This biased approach to computing dumping margins helps explain the consistently affirmative pattern of preliminary and final ITA decisions discussed in Chapter 1.

2.2.2 The Computation of Dumping Margins in Practice

Having described how the ITA determines home and U.S. market values (and thus dumping margins), I now examine how the ITA computed these margins between 1980 and 1991. Table 2-1 presents a frequency analysis of the various combinations of home and U.S. market value. For each combination, two statistics are computed. The first is the percentage of all cases in which

Table 2-1: Frequency with which the ITA uses different home and U.S. market value combinations (average dumping margins in parenthesis)

	U.S. market value				
	PP	ESP	Both PP and ESP	BIA	Overall
Home market value					
Home price	31.8% (17.8)	3.9% (33.4)	9.3% (18.3)	0.2 (47.5)	44.2% (20.6)
Third country price	5.1% (5.0)	2.0% (8.5)	1.2% (14.3)	0.2% (13.7)	8.5% (7.1)
Constructed value	10.6% (15.0)	1.5% (38.6)	2.3% (14.6)	- -	14.4% (18.8)
State-controlled economy	8.8% (26.9)	0.1% (53.2)	0.8% (19.5)	- -	9.7% (26.4)
BIA	3.0% (21.4)	- -	0.3% (42.2)	19.8% (68.7)	23.1% (62.5)
Overall	58.3% (16.1)	7.5% (32.5)	14.0% (17.2)	20.2% (67.0)	100.0% (26.3)

Source: Author's computations based on data from the *Federal Register*. See note 2 at the end of this chapter for more information.

that particular combination was used to compute the final dumping margin.[2] The second is the average dumping margin associated with that combination. In addition, the last column and the last row give, respectively, the overall frequencies with which the various definitions of home and U.S. market values were used along with the respective average dumping margins.

Consider first the overall results for home market value, contained in the last column of Table 2-1. As expected, the exporter's home price is most frequently used to compute home market value. The second most frequently used method of determining home market value is the best information available, followed by constructed value, the methods for state-controlled economies and third country prices. The highest average dumping margin is associated with the cases involving the best information available, followed by the cases involving non-market economies, home prices, constructed values and third country prices. It is not surprising that the highest average dumping margin is produced when the best information available is used to represent home market value since this information usually comes from the original petition. What is both surprising and alarming is that this method for computing home market value is the second most frequently used.

Consider next the overall results for U.S. market value, presented in the bottom row of Table 2-1. Note first that in 58% of the cases, U.S. market value is based on PP alone.[3] PP is followed in importance by the best information available, the combination of both ESP and PP, and ESP. The frequency with which the best information available is resorted to, now as a measure of U.S. market value, is again disturbing. This apprehension is raised further by noting that the average dumping margin in cases which use the best information available as a measure of U.S. market value is over twice as great as that under ESP, and over four times as great as that under PP. The fact that the dumping margins computed under ESP are on average twice as great as those under PP is also troubling, and suggests that some bias exists in the way the ESP is applied. This concern is mitigated somewhat by the fact that the ESP is used by itself in only about 8% of all cases.

Finally, consider the frequencies of the various combinations of home and U.S. market values, which are presented in the body of Table 2-1. The combination of home price and PP is the most frequently used (in nearly 32% of all cases.) This is encouraging in that these two prices are the easiest to compute and involve the fewest number of adjustments. This combination is characterized by an average dumping margin of 17.8, which is 30% lower than the overall average dumping margin of 26.3%.

Notice, however, that the second most frequently used combination (used in nearly 20% of all cases) is that in which the best information available is used to represent both home and U.S. market value. Table 2-1 indicates that in cases in which the best information available is used as a measure of both home and foreign market value, the average dumping margin is 68.7% This average is 160% greater than the overall average.

Perhaps most alarming, in recent years this combination has been used more frequently. In Table 2-2, I provide data on the use of the best information available for the years 1980 through 1991. Table 2-2 also contains, for the same years, the average overall dumping margin, the average dumping margin in cases involving the best information available, and the average dumping margin in cases not involving the best information available. Several trends in the table are obvious. First, use of the best information available increased during the period. Between 1980 and 1985, only 10% of the dumping margins were based on the best information available; between 1986 and 1991, this percentage increased to over 30%. The result has been a rapid increase in average dumping margins during the period: before 1986, the average dumping margin in any year never exceeded 20%. Since then, it has exceeded 24% in every year.

The results discussed above beg the question of why the best information available has been resorted to so frequently in recent years, both as a measure of home and U.S. market value. According to the Trade Agreements Act of 1979, the best information available is to be used

> ...whenever a party or any other person refuses or is unable to produce information requested in a timely manner and in the form required, or otherwise significantly impedes an investigation...[4]

Table 2-2: Dumping margins and the BIA, 1980-91

Year	% of margins based on BIA	Average margin	Average BIA margin	Average non-BIA margin
1980	12.9	13.8	15.4	13.3
1981	0.0	3.7	-	3.7
1982	16.6	6.8	14.0	6.5
1983	0.0	12.3	-	12.3
1984	6.6	17.9	47.2	16.6
1985	21.4	16.3	33.9	12.4
1986	18.8	30.2	68.8	22.3
1987	17.9	24.1	65.9	15.7
1988	26.9	27.4	41.4	21.0
1989	49.8	51.2	85.2	35.2
1990	39.6	28.0	43.0	15.8
1991	44.0	33.4	63.9	21.4
Overall	23.5	26.3	63.0	15.0

Source: Based on data taken from the *Federal Register*

By threatening to use the best information available, the ITA provides foreign firms with an incentive to participate in dumping investigations. Foreign firms which refuse to cooperate are usually punished severely because in most cases, the best information available is deliberately taken from information provided by the domestic industry.

Despite the high costs associated with not cooperating with ITA investigators, many foreign firms have still refused to cooperate. Why? One explanation is that foreign firms refuse to cooperate because doing so would produce a dumping margin even larger than that based on the best information available. In other words, foreign firms refuse to cooperate because they believe that the dumping margin computed by the ITA would exceed that reported in the petition. Under these circumstances, the foreign firm is better off not cooperating. While this explanation may be true in some cases, it is not likely to be true in general because the margins reported in the petition are likely to be inflated by the domestic industry.

It is more likely that foreign firms refuse to cooperate because they believe that it will be less costly to do so. Thus foreign firms do not participate in ITA investigations because they believe that the margin computed with the information they provide would not be far enough below the margin based on the best information available to justify cooperation. While no foreign firm cannot know in advance exactly what the margin computed by the ITA will be, each firm does have some idea of what the margin will be based on its own price information. Foreign firms are also aware that cooperation will involve significant legal and accounting costs and that there are biases inherent in ITA calculations which mean that dumping will almost always be found, regardless of whether or not it is taking place.

The justification for using the best information available to compute margins is clear when foreign firms refuse to participate in ITA investigations. The best information available is also used, however, when foreign firms are fully cooperative but cannot provide the requested information "in a timely manner or in the form required." Most foreign firms do try to cooperate with the ITA, but in many cases, these firms lack the facilities, the time, or the ability to provide the ITA with the information it requests. To illustrate some of the problems these firms face, consider the nature of the ITA questionnaire. This questionnaire typically exceeds one hundred pages in length, is in English, and must be submitted in English to the ITA in a computer readable format. The questionnaire requests data for all of the U.S. and home sales of the firm over a six month period and also requests data on the firm's shipping, distribution, and packaging costs. In many cases, the foreign firm must also provide comprehensive data on its costs of production. All of this data must be provided in an accounting format recognized by the U.S. government, a format which is alien to many foreign firms. Furthermore, foreign firms typically have only about 60 to 90 days to complete the petition and all the information they provide must be verifiable.[5] Obviously the burden on foreign firms in ITA investigations is large and it is understandable why many cooperative foreign firms cannot meet all of the ITA requirements.

How does this serve to explain the significant increase in the use of the best information seen in Table 2-2? The increase is probably due to several related factors. First, more foreign firms may have decided not to participate in ITA investigations because of the significant costs involved. Second, the ITA may have begun to apply more stringent informational standards in recent years. These higher standards make it more difficult and more costly for foreign firms to participate in ITA investigations and thus discourage cooperation. Third, the mix of foreign firms involved in dumping cases may have shifted. During the early and mid 1980s, most of the foreign firms involved in antidumping investigations were from developed countries and thus were in a better position to provide adequate responses to the ITA if they chose to do so. Since then, the percentage of cases involving developing countries has risen, increasing the probability that foreign firms will not be able to respond adequately because of inadequate resources. Indeed, since 1986, more than half of the cases in which the best information available was used involved developing countries.

2.2.3 Summary

In summary, the procedures used by the ITA for computing dumping margins are tainted to some extent by an increasing reliance on the best information available. It does appear that the majority of the dumping margins computed by the ITA involve fairly straightforward computations which are unlikely to produce a large bias against foreign firms. However, in a significant and increasing number of cases, dumping margins are being computed in a manner which clearly favors domestic petitioners.

2.3 The ITC and Material Injury

While the role of the ITA is to determine the extent of any dumping, the role of the ITC is to determine whether dumped imports materially injure a domestic industry. In this section, I assess the extent to which ITC material injury decisions are based on economic criteria. My analysis of these decisions differs from previous analysis in that I more rigorously model the ITC decision making process.

The ITC is an independent government agency responsible for analyzing trade policy questions, including those involving dumped imports. The ITC consists of 6 commissioners and a support staff of economists, lawyers and other personnel. The commissioners are appointed by the president and approved by congress. Under normal circumstances, each commissioner serves one 9 year term which is not renewable. The commissioners are responsible for the antidumping decisions of the ITC as well as for ITC decisions involving other trade policy matters. Each decision is based on a simple vote with the majority opinion prevailing.[6]

The role of the ITC in administering the U.S. antidumping laws is to determine whether or not the dumped imports materially injure or threaten to materially injure a U.S. industry or materially retard the development of that industry.[7] Each antidumping decision involves a preliminary ruling by the ITC on whether there is a reasonable indication that the dumped imports have caused or threaten to cause material injury. If this ruling is negative, the case is dismissed; if the ruling is affirmative, the case is passed over to the ITA, which is responsible for determining the extent of any dumping. If the ITA finds that dumping is taking place, then the ITC will render a final decision on the case. If this decision is affirmative, antidumping duties will be levied. If the ITC's final decision is negative, the case is dismissed.

What are the criteria used by the ITC commissioners to make their decisions? The criteria used by the ITC commissioners varies depending on the nature of the injury facing the domestic industry. Different criteria exist for the case in which the domestic industry is experiencing material injury and for the case in which the domestic industry is threatened with material injury.[8] In cases involving actual material injury, the commission is directed by law to consider changes in the following variables when evaluating the condition of the domestic industry: output, sales, market share, profits, productivity, capacity utilization, investment, return on investment, prices, cash flow, inventories, employment, wages, growth, and the industry's ability to raise capital. Also to be considered are any changes in the volume and value of the unfair imports, the market penetration of the unfair imports, and the price of these imports. It should be noted that each commissioner is free to examine "all relevant economic factors" in making his or her decision, and not just those mentioned above. Several commissioners have included, among other variables, the dumping margin.[9]

In cases involving the threat of material injury, the criteria set out by law include the potential for increases in foreign productive capacity, any unused foreign capacity, the likelihood of product shifting and any substantial increase in importer's inventories. Note the differences between the criteria used in cases involving actual material injury and cases involving the threat of material injury. These differences will become important later.

2.3.1 The Bifurcated and Unified Approaches

Having discussed the structure of the ITC and its role in administering the antidumping laws, consider next the methods used by the commissioners to make their decisions. There are two different methods for determining whether a domestic industry has been or is likely to be injured by dumped imports. The first approach is known as bifurcation. Bifurcation involves a two stage decision making process: first, the domestic industry must be shown to be materially injured; second, it must be shown that the dumped imports have caused or threaten to cause material injury to the domestic industry. The second approach is known as the unified or comparative approach. The unified approach does not require that the domestic industry be materially injured or threatened with material injury in the strict sense used above. Instead of examining the condition of the domestic industry, it tries to determine what would have happened if no dumping had taken place. Having made this determination, it is then possible to see the impact of the unfair imports on the domestic industry. Material injury decisions are not based on the condition of the domestic industry but rather on a comparison between the current state of the domestic industry and its hypothetical state if no dumping had taken place. Under this approach, an industry can be healthy and still receive relief if the dumped imports have weakened it substantially. In practice, the bifurcated approach dominates the unified approach. During the sample period under consideration here, decisions based on the bifurcated approach accounted for about 80% of all decisions.

I illustrate the bifurcated approach formally in Figure 2-1. The first decision required in the process is whether or not a domestic industry has been materially retarded by unfair imports. If material retardation has taken place, duties are levied. If there is no material retardation, the question of material injury to the domestic industry is addressed. If the domestic industry has suffered material injury, the question is then whether the unfair imports are the cause of material injury. If so, duties are levied. If there is no material injury to the domestic industry or if the unfair imports are not viewed as a cause of material injury, it must then be determined whether or not the unfair imports threaten material injury. If so, duties are once again levied. If not, no duties will be levied and the case will be dismissed

The unified approach, illustrated in Figure 2-2, is identical to bifurcation in regards to material retardation and the threat of material injury. It differs from the bifurcated approach only in cases involving material injury vis-a-vis unfair imports. In these cases, the unified approach differs because it does not require that the domestic industry be materially injured per se. Rather it

Figure 2-1: The bifurcated approach

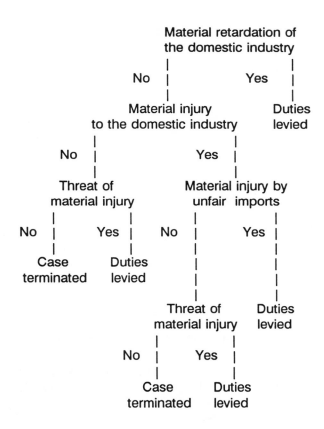

Figure 2-2: The unified approach

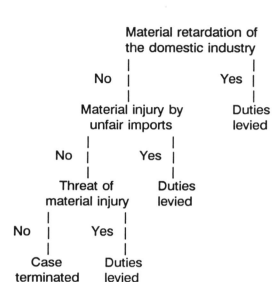

is only necessary that the unfair imports weaken the domestic industry.

The importance of modelling the ITC decision making process appropriately should now be clear. Ignoring the bifurcated approach may produce results which are misleading. Consider the following two examples. In the first example, suppose a petition is dismissed because the domestic industry is not materially injured. Under these circumstances, nothing can be said about the variables which enter the causation decision because there is no such decision. Including causation variables in these cases (as others have) is unnecessary and potentially misleading. In the second case, suppose there is material injury to the domestic industry but not as a result of the dumped or subsidized imports. Then the data on the status of the domestic industry will appear to conflict with the final decision if bifurcation is not accounted for. In both cases, ignoring bifurcation produces results which are likely to understate the importance of economic criteria.

Antidumping duties may be levied in three distinct situations. Duties will be levied if the establishment of a U.S. industry is material retarded by unfair imports, if a U.S. industry is materially injured by unfair imports, or if a U.S. industry is threatened with material injury by unfair imports. By law, each of these outcomes is based on a different set of economic criteria. In this paper, I do not attempt to focus on all three sets of criteria. Instead, I look only at the criteria used to determine whether a U.S. industry is materially injured by unfair imports. What this means is that I consider only a portion of the decision trees described in Figures 2-1 and 2-2 for each case. These portions are depicted in Figures 2-3 and 2-4 for the bifurcated and unified approaches.

Threat and retardation decisions are excluded because I want to focus on the economic criteria used most frequently, and these are the criteria which apply to material injury. Excluding decisions involving material retardation produces no real loss of generality since material retardation is an issue in only one case contained in the sample period. Excluding decisions involving the threat of material injury produces a much greater loss of generality since these decisions were much more frequent.

I illustrate the effect of discarding threat rulings in the following example. Consider a case in which a commissioner finds that a U.S. industry is not currently injured by unfair imports but is threatened with injury. In my model, the commissioner's negative vote on material injury by unfair imports is all that counts. Even though he or she ultimately voted in the affirmative on the case, the criteria used in making this affirmative decision are not the criteria that I am analyzing. The criteria I am interested in indicate no material injury by unfair imports.

2.3.2 The Data

The data employed in this paper were obtained from the final antidumping and antisubsidy reports of the ITC.[10] I have chosen to include antisubsidy cases in the sample because the procedures used by the ITC commissioners to assess material

Figure 2-3:   Partial model of the bifurcated approach

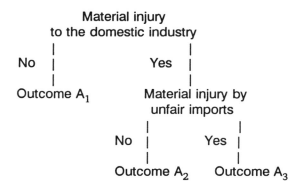

Figure 2-4: Partial model of the unified approach

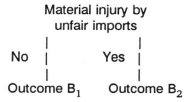

injury in antidumping and antisubsidy cases are virtually identical. Moreover, since the point of the analysis is to evaluate the way economic criteria are used by the ITC commissioners, including antisubsidy cases will allow me to reach more general conclusions.

The data in the ITC reports are derived from surveys of the domestic and foreign participants. The ITC data is the most appropriate for my purposes for two reasons. First, the data published in the ITC reports is in most cases highly disaggregated. Antidumping and antisubsidy cases involve very limited product definitions and data from other sources at the same level of disaggregation are not available on a consistent basis. Second, even if data were available from alternative sources at the same level of disaggregation, the ITC data would still be preferred because it is the data which is used by the individual commissioners to make their decisions.

The only major limitation of the ITC data is that it is kept confidential when its disclosure would involve the release of proprietary information. Typically, the ITC data is kept confidential in cases involving a single or small number of domestic or foreign firms. As a result of this confidentiality requirement, a substantial number of decisions (roughly 35%) could not be included in the econometric analysis.[11] A significant number of observations (roughly 20%) were dropped because of missing data in the final reports.

The time frame for the analysis runs from March, 1985 through December, 1990. I selected this time frame because it was in the spring of 1985 that the distinction between the bifurcated and unified approaches crystallized. Prior to the spring of 1985, it was not always possible to know which approach was being applied by a given commissioner, and thus I have chosen to exclude cases which were completed before March of 1985.

Following Moore [1990], the dependent variables represent the votes of the individual commissioners. There are compelling reasons for using the votes of the individual commissioners rather than the overall outcome of a case. First, using the overall outcome blurs the distinction between split and unanimous decisions. As a result, the economic criteria in cases involving split and unanimous decisions are treated in the same way. This equal treatment is likely to produce results which mask the importance of the economic criteria.

A second reason for using the votes of the individual commissioners is that otherwise it is impossible to know why an affirmative decision was rendered. As has already been stated, affirmative decisions can arise for three reasons: first, the domestic industry is materially injured; second, the domestic industry is threatened with material injury; third, the development of the domestic industry is being materially retarded. In each of these cases, a different set of economic criteria apply. If one looks solely at the overall outcome of a case, it is impossible to know which of these criteria is being used to support an affirmative decision.

An example is instructive here. Consider a case in which three commissioners find that a domestic industry is threatened with material injury while three commissioners find no material injury and no threat of material injury.[12] The overall outcome of such a case is affirmative (ties are decided in favor of the domestic industry.) If one is trying to measure the importance of the economic criteria for determining material injury, as I am, using the overall outcome in this case is misleading. While the overall outcome is affirmative, no commissioner has ruled that the domestic industry is materially injured. The affirmative decision arises because of the threat of material injury, which is based on a very different set of economic criteria.

A final reason for using the votes of the individual commissioners is that different commissioners view the facts of a case in different ways. Differences arise over the definitions of the products and industries involved, over the condition of the domestic industry, and over the causal connection between the unfair imports and the condition of the domestic industry. Even where there is complete agreement on all of these issues, commissioners may choose to analyze the same data in different ways.[13] If one wishes to account for these differences, there is no alternative but to examine the votes of the individual commissioners.

For all of these reasons, the dependent variable used in this study is the vote of the individual commissioner rather than the overall outcome of the case. For the bifurcated approach, there are two dependent variables, one for the material injury decision and one for the causation decision. The unified approach, by its nature, involves a single dependent variable. Appendix A contains a description of the approaches taken by each of the commissioners who served during the sample period.

I present the independent variables used in the analysis in Table 2-3. These are described in greater detail in Appendix A. The independent variables include percentage changes in profit rates, domestic and foreign market share, production, employment, domestic shipments, apparent consumption, domestic unit values and import volumes. Domestic unit values

Table 2-3: Summary of independent variables

PROF   - Domestic industry's profit rate.
SRPROF   - One year percentage change in PROF.
LRPROF   - Two year percentage change in PROF.

DMS   - Domestic industry's market share.
SRDMS   - One year percentage change in DMS.
LRDMS   - Two year percentage change in DMS.

SRPROD   - One year percentage change in production
LRPROD   - Two year percentage change in production

SRDS   - One year percentage change in shipments.
LRDS   - Two year percentage change in shipments.

SREMP   - One year percentage change in employment.
LREMP   - Two year percentage change in employment.

SRAC   - One year percentage change in consumption.
LRAC   - Two year percentage change in consumption.

FMS   - Market share of unfair imports.
SRFMS   - One year percentage change in FMS.
LRFMS   - Two year percentage change in FMS.

MARGIN   - Dumping or subsidy margin, in ad valorem terms.

SRIMP   - One year percentage change in unfair imports.
LRIMP   - Two year percentage change in unfair imports.

SRUV   - One year percentage change in U.S. unit value.
LRUV   - Two year percentage change in U.S. unit value.

are used because they represent the only domestic price data consistently available. Several commissioners state that trends in domestic prices play an important role in their decisions and while unit values are at best imperfect proxies for domestic prices, they are better than nothing.

Also included as independent variables are the most recent profit rate, the dumping or subsidy margin and the most recent domestic and foreign market shares. While none of the latter variables are named specifically in the legislation, these variables are consistently referred to in the opinions of several commissioners and one would be hard pressed to argue that they are not "relevant economic factors" and thus consistent with the legislation.[14]

2.3.3 Econometric Modelling

The data set just described could be used in one of two ways. First, the data for each commissioner could be used to fit a model for that commissioner depending upon his or her methodology. Second, the data could be pooled across the commissioners according to their methodologies and a single model could be fitted for each approach rather than for each commissioner. I have chosen to pool the data across methodologies. The main reason for this choice is that several of the commissioners cast a small number of votes during the observation period (although none less than 20.) Pooling the data across commissioners forces the parameter estimates for these commissioners to be equal, so some loss of generality is likely. To offset this loss, fixed effects were estimated for each commissioner whenever possible.[15]

I use two different econometric models to represent the two different methodologies employed by the commissioners. Since the dependent variable (commissioner vote) in both models is qualitative (affirmative or negative), logit models are appropriate for the analysis. I use a sequential logit model to estimate the parameters for the bifurcated approach. A sequential logit model is appropriate in this case because the decisions concerning material injury and causation appear to be independent in practice. Thus, the decision concerning material injury to the domestic industry is based on data for the domestic industry (i.e. production, profits, employment) while the decision concerning causation is based on data for the unfair imports (i.e. the dumping or subsidy margin, foreign market share, import volumes.)

Let X represent the vector of independent variables which summarizes the condition of the domestic industry (including any constant or fixed effects) and let Z represent the independent variables used to address the question of causation (again including any constant or fixed effects.) Using the notation for outcomes given in Figure 2-3, the probability of a negative material injury decision can be expressed as

$$2.1 \quad P(A_1 \mid X) = \frac{1}{e^{\beta X} + 1}$$

while the probability of a negative causation decision can be written as

$$2.2 \quad P(A_2 \mid X, Z) = \frac{1}{e^{\alpha Z} + 1} [1 - P(A_1)]$$

Given the independence between the material injury and causation decisions, I estimate the parameter vectors α and β by maximizing the likelihood functions of two successive dichotomous logit functions (See Amemiya [1985] or Maddala [1983] for some examples.) In the first case, I estimate the parameters relevant to the material injury decision using the entire data set. In the second case, I estimate the parameters relevant to the causation decision using the subset of cases in which material injury is present.

I use a simple logit model to estimate the parameters for the unified approach. Using the notation of Figure 2-4, the probability of a negative unified decision can be expressed as

$$2.3 \quad P(B_1 \mid X, Z) = \frac{1}{e^{\beta X + \alpha Z} + 1}$$

Estimates of the two parameter vectors are obtained by maximizing the associated likelihood function.

2.3.4 Results

Before I discuss the logit results, I provide some descriptive statistics. Tables 2-4 and 2-5 contain the means and medians of the independent variables conditioned upon the procedure used and the commissioner's vote. Consider Table 2-4 first, which lists the conditional means and medians of the independent variables under bifurcation. The top portion of Table 2-4 focuses on the material injury decision. If commissioners base their decisions upon economic criteria, affirmative decisions should have lower means and medians than negative decisions. This is because higher values of the independent variables indicate that the domestic industry is not as likely to be suffering material injury. A glance at the top half of Table 2-4 reveals that the affirmative means and medians are lower than their negative counterparts in all but 2 of a possible 28 cases. This is evidence that economic criteria do matter, at least in determining material injury.

The lower half of Table 2-4 examines the second half of the bifurcated decision, which involves the causal link between dumped or subsidized imports and the material injury suffered by the domestic industry. We would expect that commissioners who use economic criteria would be more likely to render an affirmative decision the higher is the dumping/subsidy margin, the higher is the market share of the dumped or subsidized imports, the more rapid is the rate of increase in the volume and market share of the dumped or subsidized imports, and the smaller is the rate of increase in domestic unit values. Examining the lower half of Table 2-4, we find that the results are mixed. The data support the conclusion that the dumping/subsidy margin and the market share of the dumped or subsidized imports are used appropriately in determining causality. The remaining economic variables do not exhibit patterns consistent with the legislation.

Table 2-4: Conditional means and medians for bifurcated decisions (A - affirmative decision, N - negative decision)

Variable	Conditional mean		Conditional median	
	A	N	A	N
Material injury criteria (531 observations)				
DMS	63.8	71.9	69.3	76.0
SRDMS	-2.3	-3.5	-3.0	-2.3
LRDMS	-7.7	-5.6	-5.0	-6.7
PROF	1.0	7.9	1.4	3.1
SRPROF	33.7	138.6	-5.6	8.8
LRPROF	-43.1	25.6	-23.0	-9.0
SRAC	2.1	10.3	-0.1	3.2
LRAC	9.6	21.3	9.1	10.2
SRDS	-0.8	4.6	-0.7	3.5
LRDS	1.3	11.4	-7.2	8.6
SREMP	-3.3	0.5	-2.9	1.8
LREMP	-3.0	-1.4	-7.5	3.6
SRPROD	-2.0	4.4	-0.9	2.3
LRPROD	3.6	9.7	-6.5	11.5
Causation criteria (320 observations)				
MARGIN	34.6	16.8	18.2	7.9
FMS	26.0	11.9	23.8	5.7
SRFMS	41.0	385.3	6.3	19.3
LRFMS	102.2	896.5	17.8	63.4
SRIMP	45.4	376.7	11.4	19.8
LRIMP	131.1	1052.4	12.3	90.0
SRUV	-1.0	-1.1	-2.5	-2.5
LRUV	-1.2	-1.2	-0.5	-0.2

Table 2-5: Conditional means and medians for unified decisions
(A - affirmative decision, N - negative decision)

Variable	Conditional Mean		Conditional Median	
	A	N	A	N
Material Injury				
Criteria (126 Observations)				
DMS	59.0	62.4	61.0	72.1
SRDMS	-0.8	0.1	0.4	-1.5
LRDMS	-9.4	-5.1	-7.4	-5.1
PROF	1.3	4.5	0.7	3.0
SRPROF	86.8	239.4	65.6	15.4
LRPROF	67.6	43.0	81.8	61.7
SRAC	6.5	3.0	-1.4	0.8
LRAC	27.5	11.8	15.7	9.8
SRDS	3.3	2.9	3.3	1.7
LRDS	12.9	5.1	8.6	2.9
SREMP	1.7	-1.9	-1.2	-2.9
LREMP	10.6	-4.3	9.6	-7.6
SRPROD	6.5	2.9	7.5	1.9
LRPROD	25.4	4.2	12.0	5.9
Causation				
Criteria (126 observations)				
MARGIN	29.6	31.3	22.0	17.1
FMS	26.1	19.0	24.1	12.0
SRFMS	252.9	212.5	28.9	17.8
LRFMS	476.0	929.9	56.9	14.4
SRIMP	278.8	214.5	21.7	3.3
LRIMP	600.1	1141.5	105.3	11.2
SRUV	-0.7	2.6	-3.3	2.8
LRUV	-2.7	3.2	0.6	0.1

Consider next Table 2-5, which presents the conditional means and medians of the independent variables under the unified approach. The interpretation of these means and medians differs from that under bifurcation because the unified approach focuses on the extent of any injury caused by the unfair imports, and not on the status of the domestic industry. Thus we would not expect the conditional means and medians of the material injury variables to take on any particular pattern. Examining the top half of Table 2-5, it can be seen that the material injury criteria receive little weight, which is to be expected under the unified approach.

Because the unified approach focuses largely on the extent of any injury, we would expect that the independent variables which are important in assessing causality would take on the same patterns expected under bifurcation. The lower half of Table 2-5 shows that the expected pattern holds true for 12 of the 16 comparisons, and this is weak evidence that the causality criteria are used appropriately under the unified approach.

Having examined the conditional means and medians of the independent variables, consider next the logit results, presented in Tables 2-6 through 2-8. Tables 2-6 and 2-7 present the results for the bifurcated approach while Table 2-8 presents the results for the unified approach. I consider the results for the bifurcated approach first.

Table 2-6 contains the logit results for the first half of the bifurcated decision, which focuses on the question of material injury to the domestic industry. Since all of the independent variables are positively related to the health of the domestic industry, one would expect that an increase in any of the independent variables would increase the likelihood of a negative decision if these variables are used by the ITC in its assessment of material injury. Examination of equation 2.1 reveals that this will be the case only if the elements of the parameter vector β are negative. Thus, the hypothesis that the independent variables are important determinants in bifurcated material injury decisions will be supported if the coefficients presented in Table 2-6 are negative.

Examination of Table 2-6 reveals that 26 of the 32 coefficients are negative. Of the 26 coefficients which have the

Table 2-6: Logit results for bifurcated decisions involving material injury (standard errors in parenthesis)

	Model			
Variable	1	2	3	4
Constant	2.45***	-	2.46***	-
	(0.48)	-	(0.54)	-
Fixed effects				
BRUNSDALE	-	0.63	-	0.78
	-	(0.65)	-	(0.67)
ECKES	-	3.47***	-	3.3***
	-	(0.58)	-	(0.62)
LIEBELER	-	1.23	-	1.5**
	-	(0.66)	-	(0.67)
LODWICK	-	2.57***	-	2.4***
	-	(0.56)	-	(0.60)
NEWQUIST	-	3.86***	-	3.5***
	-	(0.71)	-	(0.74)
ROHR	-	2.54***	-	2.5***
	-	(0.55)	-	(0.59)
Independent variables				
PROF	0.15***	-0.20***	-0.12***	-0.2***
	(0.02)	(0.02)	(0.02)	(0.02)
SRPROF	-0.0008*	-0.001*	-	-
	(0.0004)	(0.0006)	-	-
LRPROF	-	-	-0.002**	-0.1***
	-	-	(0.001)	(0.001)
DMS	-0.016***	-0.016**	-0.021***	-0.1***
	(0.006)	(0.007)	(0.007)	(0.007)
SRDMS	-0.046*	-0.053*	-	-
	(0.027)	(0.029)	-	-
LRDMS	-	-	-0.065**	-0.06**
	-	-	(0.033)	(0.032)

Table 2-6 (continued)

SREMP	0.0018	-0.021	-	-
	(0.0143)	(0.016)	-	-
LREMP	-	-	0.008	-0.002
	-	-	(0.010)	(0.010)
SRPROD	-0.105***	-0.125***	-	-
	(0.023)	(0.026)	-	-
LRPROD	-	-	0.017	0.019
	-	-	(0.012)	(0.013)
SRDS	0.075**	0.082**	-	-
	(0.029)	(0.033)	-	-
LRDS	-	-	-0.129	-0.022
	-	-	(0.012)	(0.030)
SRAC	-0.046**	-0.038	-	-
	(0.022)	(0.023)	-	-
LRAC	-	-	-0.039	-0.028
	-	-	(0.025)	(0.024)
Log likelihood	-266.5	-238.0	-269.1	-246.6
% of correct predictions	74.0	82.7	75.1	81.9
Number of observations	531	531	531	531

*,**,*** - Significant at 10%, 5% and 1% levels respectively.

The Efficacy of Antidumping Duties

Table 2-7: Logit results for bifurcated decisions involving causality
(standard errors in parenthesis)

Variable	1	Model 2	3	4
Constant	-0.056	-	-0.063	-
	(0.298)	-	(0.321)	-
Fixed effects				
BRUNSDALE	-	-1.082*	-	-1.1*
	-	(0.585)	-	(0.583)
ECKES	-	0.545	-	0.8*
	-	(0.441)	-	(0.475)
LIEBELER	-	-2.910***	-	-2.8***
	-	(0.691)	-	(0.687)
LODWICK	-	0.645	-	0.7
	-	(0.498)	-	(0.513)
NEWQUIST	-	0.417	-	0.4
	-	(0.715)	-	(0.724)
ROHR	-	0.770	-	0.8
	-	(0.513)	-	(0.532)
Independent variables				
MARGIN	0.018***	0.019**	0.020***	0.02**
	(0.007)	(0.008)	(0.007)	(0.009)
FMS	0.060***	0.060***	0.061***	0.1***
	(0.013)	(0.016)	(0.014)	(0.016)
SRFMS	-0.015**	-0.016**	-	-
	(0.008)	(0.008)	-	-
LRFMS	-	-	-0.004	-0.001
	-	-	(0.003)	(0.003)
SRIMP	0.014*	0.015*	-	-
	(0.008)	(0.008)	-	-
LRIMP	-	-	0.003	0.001
	-	-	(0.003)	(0.003)
SRUV	-0.010	-0.028*	-	-
	(0.015)	(0.016)	-	-

Table 2-7 (continued)

LRUV	-	-	0.012	-0.016
	-	-	(0.016)	(0.018)
Log likelihood	-125.8	-100.9	-125.7	-99.5
% of correct predictions	82.2	88.1	82.2	89.1
Observations	320	320	320	320

*,**,*** - Significant at 10%, 5% and 1% levels respectively.

correct sign, 17 are significant at the 10% level, 15 are significant at the 5% level, and 10 are significant at the 1% level. The variables which are the most significant in bifurcated material injury decisions are the domestic industry's profit rate, its market share and the short run change in its production. Of the 6 coefficients which have the wrong sign, two are significant at the 5% level. Both of these coefficients show that a short run increase in domestic shipments reduces the chance of a negative decision. I am at a loss as to how to explain this result, which is clearly inconsistent with the unfair trade legislation.

With the 2 exceptions just noted, the logit results in Table 2-6 indicate that bifurcated material injury determinations are based on economic variables consistent with the unfair trade legislation. Examination of the fixed effects presented in Table 2-6 shows, however, that the threshold for material injury varies across commissioners. According to my results, Commissioners Brunsdale and Liebeler have higher injury thresholds than the other commissioners.

Table 2-7 contains the results for the second half of the bifurcated decision, which involves assessing whether unfair imports are a cause of material injury to the domestic industry. If the ITC's causality decisions are consistent with the legislation, we would expect that short and long run increases in the volume and market share of the unfair imports would reduce the probability of a negative decision while short and long run increases in domestic unit values would increase this probability. Increases in the dumping/subsidy margin and the market share of the unfair imports should also reduce the probability of a negative decision.

Combining the previous discussion with equation 2.2, the hypothesis that the ITC uses economic criteria appropriately in its bifurcated causality decisions will be supported if the coefficients on MARGIN, FMS, SRFMS, LRFMS, SRIMP, and LRIMP are positive and if the coefficients on SRUV and LRUV are negative. Examining the coefficients on the independent variables presented in Table 2-7, it can be seen that 15 of the 20 coefficients have the correct sign. Of those coefficients which have the correct sign, 11 are significant at the 10% level, 8 are significant at the 5% percent level and 6 are significant at the 1% level. The variables which are most important in causality decisions are the dumping/subsidy margin and the market share of the unfair imports.[16] Of the 5 coefficients which have the wrong sign, two are significant at the 5% level. Both of these coefficients show that a short run increase in foreign market share increases the probability of a negative decision. This result is clearly inconsistent with the unfair trade legislation.

With the two exceptions just noted, the logit results for the causality decision support the hypothesis that economic criteria are important in determining causality. Examination of the fixed effects suggests that most commissioners share the same standard for causation. Only one of the commissioners (Liebeler) appears to have a significantly different standard for causation. Her standard appears to be much higher than that of the other commissioners. In summary, the logit results, with a few exceptions, strongly support the hypothesis that economic criteria do matter in bifurcated decisions.

Table 2-8 contains the logit results for cases involving the unified approach. Before examining these results, remember that the unified approach does not require that a domestic industry be suffering material injury per se. A healthy domestic industry may still receive relief if the unfair imports have weakened it

Table 2-8: Logit Results for Unified Decisions (standard errors in parenthesis)

Variable	1	2	3	4
Constant	1.077	-10.654**	-19.9***	-15.1**
	(3.451)	(4.970)	(6.37)	(6.77)
Fixed Effects				
BRUNSDALE	-	1.866	-	4.45
	-	(1.717)	-	(2.83)
STERN	-	7.139***	-	8.6**
	-	(2.427)	-	(4.03)
Variables related to material injury				
PROF	0.093	0.050	0.247**	0.030
	(0.061)	(0.069)	(0.12)	(0.134)
SRPROF	0.004***	0.004**	-	-
	(0.001)	(0.002)	-	-
LRPROF	-	-	0.038***	0.04**
	-	-	(0.013)	(0.014)
DMS	-0.078*	-0.009	0.101**	0.09*
	(0.046)	(0.048)	(0.045)	(0.055)
SRDMS	0.093	-0.003	-	-
	(0.106)	(0.078)	-	-
LRDMS	-	-	-0.130	0.598
	-	-	(0.206)	(0.440)
SREMP	0.132	0.004	-	-
	(0.088)	(0.076)	-	-
LREMP	-	-	-0.154	-0.001
	-	-	(0.121)	(0.115)
SRPROD	0.388***	0.544***	-	-
	(0.120)	(0.174)	-	-
LRPROD	-	-	0.478**	0.38**
	-	-	(0.213)	(0.183)
SRDS	-0.586***	-0.466***	-	-
	(0.161)	(0.163)	-	-

Table 2-8: (continued)

LRDS	-	-	-0.772**	-1.26**
	-	-	(0.338)	(0.569)
SRAC	0.117*	-0.111	-	-
	(0.061)	(0.093)	-	-
LRAC	-	-	-0.285	0.58*
	-	-	(0.178)	(0.309)
Variables related to causation				
MARGIN	-0.001	0.015	0.005	0.003
	(0.011)	(0.016)	(0.013)	(0.017)
FMS	0.072*	0.132***	0.165**	0.090
	(0.040)	(0.050)	(0.072)	(0.065)
SRFMS	-0.046**	-0.055***	-	-
	(0.019)	(0.021)	-	-
LRFMS	-	-	0.048**	0.04*
	-	-	(0.023)	(0.022)
SRIMP	0.043**	0.055***	-	-
	(0.018)	(0.021)	-	-
LRIMP	-	-	-0.041**	-0.03*
	-	-	(0.019)	(0.019)
SRUV	-0.735***	-0.541***	-	-
	(0.207)	(0.204)	-	-
LRUV	-	-	-0.279*	-0.45**
	-	-	(0.145)	(0.199)
Log likelihood	-29.4	-19.0	-21.7	-15.1
% of correct predictions	96.0	97.6	96.8	96.0
Number of Observations	126	126	126	126

*,**,*** - Significant at 10%, 5% and 1% levels respectively.

significantly. Given these comments, it is unlikely that the variables which reflect the status of the domestic industry will be as significant in unified decisions as they were in bifurcated decisions. Examination of Table 2-8 confirms this. Only 13 of the 32 coefficients on the variables relating to material injury have the correct sign and only 4 of these are statistically significant. Perhaps most surprising is the fact that 13 of the coefficients related to material injury are significantly positive. This suggests that healthy domestic industries are more likely to receive relief than industries which are weak. While this result may seem perverse, it is not inconsistent with the unified approach.

While the health of the domestic industry in and of itself is not particularly important in unified decisions, the causal link between the unfair imports and any decline in the industry's health is crucial. Thus a domestic industry with a profit rate of 15% may still receive relief if the unfair imports can be shown to have reduced the profit rate of the industry from 30% to 15%. These comments suggest that the variables related to causation should be highly significant in unified decisions. Inspection of the causation coefficients in Table 2-8 reveals that this is only true to a limited extent. Of the 20 coefficients, 15 have the right sign, and of these, 11 are significant at the 10% level, 8 are significant at the 5% level and 4 are significant at the 1% level. The causation variables which are the most important are the short run change in domestic prices and the short run change in unfair import volumes.

Of the 5 causation coefficients which have the wrong sign, 4 are significant. This evidence suggests that the unified approach does not rely as strongly on trends in the economic data as the bifurcated approach. This is not a surprising result since the commissioners who have used the unified approach have repeatedly rejected the trend analysis used in most bifurcated decisions. These commissioners have relied instead on elasticity estimates and/or computer simulations.[17] To properly assess the unified approach, the elasticity estimates and computer simulations need to be analyzed. Unfortunately, this information is not generally available to the public.

2.3.5 Summary

In summarizing the results of this section, remember that decisions involving bifurcation account for roughly 80% of all the decisions in the sample. Because of this, the results pertaining to bifurcation should be weighted more heavily. These results strongly support the hypothesis that ITC decisions are based on an analysis of economic variables and trends. The results for the unified approach do not support this hypothesis as strongly, but because the unified approach focuses less on economic trends, this does not mean that commissioners who have used the unified approach have ignored economic criteria. A more detailed analysis of unified decisions is necessary before any conclusions can be reached about the role of economics in these decisions.

2.4 Conclusion

This chapter examines the administration of the U.S. antidumping laws by analyzing the administrative roles of the ITA and the ITC. The results for the ITA show that dumping margins averaged about 26% between 1980 and 1991. In addition, the average dumping margin grew significantly during this period. An important factor in explaining both the size of the average margin and its growth is the significant increase in the use of the best information available, one of the means used to compute dumping margins. Dumping margins based exclusively on the best information available accounted for roughly 20% of all margins computed between 1980 and 1991 and roughly 30% of all margins computed between 1986 and 1991. While the use of the best information available is understandable in some cases (those in which foreign firms refuse to cooperate), a significant number of foreign firms, through no fault of their own, have been unjustly punished not because they were uncooperative but rather because they could not produce the necessary information in the form or the time specified by the ITA.

The results of this chapter also demonstrate that economic criteria play a significant role in the ITC's decision making process. The results obtained here indicate that certain economic variables or trends are crucial in bifurcated decisions. The economic variables and trends considered in this chapter are less relevant in ITC decisions based on the unified approach, but this is not unexpected because these decisions are usually based on other economic criteria which are not readily available for analysis. My results do not imply that economic variables are the sole or even most important determinants of ITC decisions. Because I do not control for political or political-economic variables which might influence ITC decisions, I cannot pin-point the impact of these other variables. My results do imply, however, that the ITC decision making process is not completely arbitrary and that industries are not assured of protection simply because they wield political clout. While non-economic factors may influence ITC decisions, they are not the only determinants of these decisions.

Notes

1. Third country prices will normally be selected over constructed values if there are adequate sales in the third country at prices above cost.

2. Before the percentages in Table 2-1 could be computed, it was first necessary to generate frequencies for each of the different definitions of home and U.S. market value. Unfortunately, many cases involved more than one definition of home or U.S. market value, making it unclear as to how the necessary frequencies should be computed. In these cases, the following procedure was used to compute the frequencies. If multiple definitions of home market value were used in a case, each definition received equal weight, with the sum of the weights being equal to one. This last requirement was made in order to insure that the frequencies from cases involving multiple definitions were not given disproportionate weight when combined with the frequencies from the cases involving a single definition. The same procedure was employed in cases involving multiple definitions of U.S. market value.

Cases involving multiple firms and multiple definitions of home or U.S. market value were treated as follows. In each case, each firm received equal weight, with the weights again summing to one. When a single definition was used for a particular firm, the contribution towards the overall frequency for that definition was just given by the firm's weight. In cases involving multiple definitions for a single firm, the weight of the firm was divided equally amongst the different definitions.

An example will illustrate the procedure. Consider a case involving three firms (1,2,3), two definitions of home market value (A,B), and a single definition of U.S. market value (Z). The ITA uses the A definition of home market value for firms 1 and 2 and the A and B definitions for firm 3. Using the above procedure, the contribution to the overall frequencies for definitions A and B of home market value would be 5/6 and 1/6, respectively. The contribution to the frequency of definition Z of U.S. market value would be 1. While the procedure is arbitrary, it was felt to be the most reasonable alternative. Discarding all of the cases involving multiple definitions of home or U.S. market value would have resulted in a significant loss of information.

3.   In some cases, sales of an imported product were made to both related and unrelated parties, so that U.S. market value was based on both PP and ESP.

4.   USITC pub. #1760, pp. 247-8.

5.   The information provided must be verified by the ITA deadline. Verification itself can become time consuming because it frequently requires on site inspection of production facilities. If information cannot be verified before the ITA's deadline, the best information available may be used instead.

6.   In the case of a tie, the affirmative opinion prevails.

7.   Material injury is defined as "harm which is not inconsequential, immaterial or unimportant".

8.   No specific criteria for material retardation are specified in the Trade Agreements Act of 1979. But there is no doubt that the criteria for material retardation differ from the criteria used in cases involving actual material injury or the threat of material injury. This is because material retardation cases involve industries which have not yet been established.

9.   The use of dumping margins has generated considerable controversy. The United States Court of International Trade ruled in 1987 that the ITC is not legally bound to use margins or legally prohibited from doing so (see Palmeter [1987b] for more details). This ruling apparently gives eac..

commissioner discretion in deciding whether or not margins are relevant in a particular case.

10. I focus here on the final decisions of the ITC because the preliminary decisions of the ITC are based on whether or not there is a "reasonable indication" of material injury. Because the injury threshold is lower at the preliminary level, combining the preliminary and final decisions of the ITC is likely to produce results which understate the importance of the economic criteria.

11. The extent to which the omitted data biases the results obtained here is difficult to judge. Moore [1990] shows that the percentage of cases affirmed is roughly the same whether the data is confidential or not. He also argues that because the sampling process is exogenous, the bias is likely to be small.

12. This is not a hypothetical situation. See, for example, Certain Welded Carbon Steel Pipes and Tubes from Turkey and Thailand, USITC pub. 1810.

13. For example, commissioners may use data at different levels of aggregation or may choose to cumulate imports in different ways.

14. I have not included in the study a number of variables specified in the legislation. In most cases, this is because reporting of these variables was spotty. One variable which was regularly reported but omitted nonetheless was the rate of capacity utilization. There are three reasons for this omission. First, capacity utilization rates are at best imperfect indicators of the state of an industry. This is particularly true in declining industries, where increases in capacity utilization rates often take place because of declines in productive capacity. These declines are usually the result of firms exiting an industry. Second, capacity utilization rates are difficult to define in a number of industries. This is particularly true in the steel industry, which accounts for a number of the cases included in the study. Third, capacity utilization rates are not usually available for most agricultural products, so that cases involving these products would have had to been dropped from the study.

15. In some cases, fixed effects could not be estimated because there was no variation in a commissioner's votes.

16. The significance of the dumping or subsidy margin is somewhat surprising. This is because 4 of the 6 commissioners who offered bifurcated decisions during the sample period have disavowed the use of margins in determining causality. The significance of the dumping or subsidy margin might be explained on the grounds that these 4 commissioners attach considerable weight to the margin by which the unfair imports undersell the domestic product. Because the dumping or subsidy margin probably serves as a reasonable proxy for the margin of underselling, it is not surprising that these margins are significant. Unfortunately, this hypothesis cannot be tested because the margin of underselling is rarely reported.

17. Kaplan provides a good overview of the methods used in unified decisions.

Part II: Models of Antidumping Duties

In the second part of the book, I construct both theoretical and empirical models of antidumping duties. The purpose of these models is to analyze the impact that antidumping duties have on domestic firms and domestic welfare. The models are also used to examine the impact that an alternative trade policy has on these same variables. The effects of this policy are then compared with those produced by the antidumping duty. This comparison makes it possible to assess whether antidumping duties are an effective means of providing protection to a domestic industry.

Chapter 3: A Theoretical Model of Efficacy

3.1 Introduction

In this chapter, I construct a theoretical model of antidumping duties. I then use the model to evaluate the efficacy of antidumping duties. The efficacy of antidumping duties is determined by comparing the effects of the duty with the effects of an alternative trade policy. The antidumping duty is more effective than the alternative trade policy when it provides a greater amount of relief to the domestic industry for a given reduction in domestic welfare.

The alternative trade policy used in this chapter can be thought of as a safeguard as defined in the GATT. A safeguard represents a non-discriminatory tariff or quota which is used to provide relief to a weak domestic industry facing import competition. I assume that the safeguard takes the form of a non-discriminatory tariff.[1] The main reason for choosing this trade policy as a point of comparison is that safeguards and antidumping duties have become viewed as substitutes for one another. Norall [1986], Hoekman and Leidy [1989], and Finger and Murray [1990] have all argued that antidumping duties have effectively replaced safeguards as a means of obtaining relief from import competition. This is because under the GATT, safeguards give foreign governments a legal right to retaliate while antidumping duties do not. As a result, a discriminatory tariff such as an antidumping duty may be superior to a non-discriminatory tariff if the latter involves foreign retaliation. This may be true even when the discriminatory antidumping duty produces trade diversion.

The model developed in this chapter uses a monopolistically competitive framework. Such a framework is conducive to the goals of the analysis. Two other approaches have been used to model dumping in imperfectly competitive industries. The first involves price setting oligopolistic firms. Prusa [1987] and Staiger and Wolak [1989] show that in this framework, the introduction of an antidumping mechanism can lead to higher prices and a reduction in domestic welfare even when an antidumping duty is not imposed. This is because domestic firms can threaten an antidumping suit, and this discourages foreign firms from engaging in price competition. The second alternative is the reciprocal dumping model of Brander and Krugman [1983]. In this model, quantity setting firms have an incentive, based on segmented markets, to dump in the markets of their rivals.

The model is also a partial equilibrium model. Partial equilibrium analysis is particularly appropriate in this context because antidumping duties are usually applied to products with very limited definitions. As a result, the effect of these duties on the rest of the economy will be negligible in most cases.

The remainder of the chapter is divided into five sections. In the first three sections, I describe industry structure, the pattern of trade, preferences and production in that order. In the fourth section of the chapter, I compute the effects of the antidumping duty and the non-discriminatory tariff. I then rank the two tariffs by comparing the amount of relief received by the domestic industry for a given reduction in domestic welfare. The final section summarizes the results of the chapter.

3.2 Industry Structure and the Pattern of Trade

In this section, I describe industry structure and the pattern of trade. The model involves three countries, each containing an arbitrary number of firms. Each firm produces a single product variety. In addition, firms located in the same country are assumed to be symmetric in the sense that they share the same technology and face the same demand functions. These assumptions imply that firms located in the same country produce the same quantity of output and charge the same price.

In the traditional model of dumping, a firm has a monopoly in its home market but faces competition in its export market. The higher elasticity of demand it faces in its export market leads the firm to charge a lower price in that market and the result is dumping. I extend this model in two ways: first, I allow for three countries rather than two; second, I assume that the industry is characterized by monopolistic competition. Thus entry will take place in each country until profits are zero.

Let the first country be the country which imposes the antidumping duty. As in the traditional model, this country produces output solely for domestic consumption. The second country produces output both for domestic consumption and for export to the first country. The third country produces output for its home market and for export to both the first and second countries.

The elasticity of demand in each country reflects the degree of competition in that country. Thus the first country has the highest elasticity of demand while the third country has the lowest. The result of this pattern of demand elasticities is dumping by foreign firms in both the first and second countries. Firms in the third country dump in both the first and second countries while firms in the second country dump only in the first country. I assume that only the first country levies an antidumping duty, and that it levies this duty only against exports from the third country. This assumption is justified because the difference in demand elasticities is greatest between the first and third countries. Thus the degree of price discrimination or dumping is also greatest between these two countries.

3.3 Preferences

Given these assumptions, consider the utility function of a representative agent from country j. I assume this function takes the form

$$(3.1) \quad U_j = e_j + \left(\sum_{k=1}^{3} N_k X_{kj}^{1/\mu_j} \right)^{\mu_j}$$

where X_{kj} is the consumption of any of the varieties produced in k and sold in j, N_k is the number of varieties produced in k, and e_j is the representative agent's expenditure on all other goods. This utility function attributes to consumers a love of variety which is typical of Dixit-Stiglitz type preferences. In particular, given a constant level of expenditure on the product group, utility will be increasing in the number of varieties consumed.[2] The utility function is also convenient for partial equilibrium analysis because it implies that the marginal utility of income is equal to one.

The demand functions associated with these preferences are of the form

$$(3.2) \quad X_{ij} = [P_{ij} (1 + t_{ij})]^{-b_j - 1} [l_j - e_j] /$$

$$\left\{ \sum_{k=1}^{3} N_k [P_{kj} (1 + t_{kj})]^{-b_j} \right\}$$

where P_{kj} is the price of any variety produced in k and sold in j, t_{kj} is the ad valorem tariff (if any) imposed by country j on imports from country k and l_j is country j's income. I assume that the industry under consideration is small relative to the rest of the economy so any income effects can be ignored. The parameter $b_j + 1$ gives the absolute value of the elasticity of substitution for consumers in country j. It is also approximately equal to the price elasticity of demand in country j.[3]

Equilibrium will be reached in the goods market when the supply and demand for each variety are equated, or when

$$(3.3) \quad X_k = \sum_{j=1}^{3} X_{kj} \qquad\qquad k = 1, 2, 3$$

where X_k is the total output of any firm in k. Log differentiating the goods market equilibrium conditions, we find that

$$(3.4) \quad \mathbf{X_k} = - \sum_{j=1}^{3} \sigma_{kj} \left[(b_j + 1) (\mathbf{P_{kj}} + \mathbf{t_{kj}}) + \mathbf{D_j} \right]$$

$$\text{where} \quad \mathbf{D_j} = \sum_{i=1}^{3} \phi_{ij} \left[\mathbf{N_i} - b_j (\mathbf{P_{ij}} + \mathbf{t_{ij}}) \right]$$

$$\sigma_{kj} = X_{kj} / X_k$$

$$\phi_{ij} = N_i P_{ij} X_{ij} / \sum_{l=1}^{3} N_l P_{lj} X_{lj}$$

where variables in bold print represent proportional changes. The parameter σ_{kj} gives the fraction of total output sold in country j by any firm located in country k. The parameter ϕ_{ij} gives the market share of the ith country in the jth market. The assumptions made earlier about market structure imply that

$$\sigma_{12} = \sigma_{13} = \sigma_{23} = 0 \qquad \sigma_{11} = 1$$

$$\phi_{12} = \phi_{13} = \phi_{23} = 0 \qquad \phi_{33} = 1$$

$$b_1 > b_2 > b_3$$

The absence of income effects implies that changes in a given tariff rate affect welfare through changes in consumer surplus and the tariff revenue. The use of consumer surplus is valid here because the marginal utility of income is constant. Consumer surplus in country j can be written as

$$(3.5) \quad CS = \left(\sum_{k=1}^{3} N_k X_{kj} \right)^{1/\mu_j} \mu_j - \sum_{k=1}^{3} N_k P_{kj} (1 + t_{kj}) X_{kj}$$

Adding the tariff revenue to (3.5) and log differentiating yields the following expression for the change in welfare in country j

$$(3.6) \quad W_j = A_j \, D_j + B_j \sum_{k=1}^{3} \phi_{kj} \, t_{kj}$$

where A_j and B_j are positive constants which vary across j. This expression has a simple interpretation: the first term on the right hand side represents the change in consumer surplus while the second term represents the change in the tariff revenue.

3.4 Production

Given the industry structure and preferences described in the previous section, consider next the firm's production technology and its maximization problem. Let the cost function of any firm located in k be

$$(3.7) \quad C_k = F_k + c_k \, X_k$$

where F_k is the cost of entry in country k and c_k is the marginal cost of any firm producing in k. I assume that $c_1 > c_2 > c_3$. This assumption is consistent with the pattern of trade, but more importantly, it mirrors the situation in which most antidumping duties are imposed.

Given this technology, a firm in k solves

$$\underset{X_{kj}}{\text{Max}} \quad \sum_{j=1}^{3} P_{kj} \, X_{kj} - C_k$$

The first order conditions are of the form

$$(3.8) \quad P_{kj} = \mu_j \, c_k$$

The parameter μ_j, which was introduced in the last section, has a different interpretation in this context. It now represents the "monopoly power" of any firm with sales in country j, where monopoly power is defined as the ratio of average revenue to marginal revenue. For example, the assumption that demand is more elastic in the first country implies that $\mu_3 > \mu_1$ so firms in the third country receive a greater markup in their home market than they do in the first country. Log differentiating the first order condition yields equations of the form

(3.9) $P_{kj} = P_k = 0$

In the long run, the number of firms located in a particular country is determined by a zero profit condition. Using the firm's first order conditions, this zero profit condition can be expressed in the following form[4]

(3.10) $\displaystyle\sum_{j=1}^{3} \mu_j \sigma_{kj} = \theta_k$

where the left hand side represents a weighted average of the monopoly power of a firm located in k and the right hand side represents the inverse of the elasticity of the cost function, a standard measure of scale economies. Log differentiating this condition yields

(3.11) $\displaystyle\sum_{j=1}^{3} \mu_j \sigma_{kj} X_{kj} = X_k$

3.5 Results

Before discussing the results, I first must define what is meant by relief in this chapter. According to U.S. antidumping law, two conditions must be met before an antidumping duty can be imposed. First, dumping must be present. Second, dumping must be the cause of material injury to a domestic industry. Several factors are important in determining whether or not a domestic industry has been injured by dumping. One of these factors is the change in the industry's output. In order to achieve a measure of congruence between the injury caused by the dumping and the relief provided by the antidumping duty, I will limit my definition of relief to include only changes in domestic output. The output of the domestic industry is affected by both changes in output per firm and changes in the number of varieties produced domestically (i.e. changes in the number of domestic firms.)

Having defined relief, the changes in product variety, output and welfare brought about by an antidumping duty are now solved for. Using equations (3.4), (3.9), and (3.10), the changes in each country's output per firm and its number of firms are given by[5]

(3.12) $X_{1ad} = 0$

(3.13) $X_{2ad} = 0$

(3.14) $X_{3ad} = \mu_1 \, \sigma_{31} \, (b_3 - b_1) \, t_{ad} < 0$

(3.15) $N_{1ad} = \dfrac{b_3 \sigma_{31} \mu_1 (\phi_{31}\phi_{22} - \phi_{32}\phi_{21}) + b_1 \sigma_{33}\phi_{31}\phi_{22}}{\sigma_{33} \, \phi_{11} \, \phi_{22}} \, t_{ad} > 0$

(3.16) $N_{2ad} = \dfrac{\sigma_{31}\phi_{32}}{\sigma_{33}\phi_{22}} \, b_3 \, \mu_1 \, t_{ad} > 0$

(3.17) $N_{3ad} = -\dfrac{\sigma_{31}}{\sigma_{33}} \, b_3 \, \mu_1 \, t_{ad} < 0$

These results show that total output in both the first and second countries rises as a result of the antidumping duty, and that this rise is due entirely to an influx of new firms. Conversely, total output declines in the third country as a result of both firm exit and a decline in output per firm.

The amount of relief obtained by the domestic industry as a result of the antidumping duty will depend on several factors. Perhaps most important, the amount of relief provided by the antidumping duty will be decreasing in ϕ_{32}, which is the market share of the third country's firms in the second country. It is this market share parameter which in large part determines the extent of any trade diversion. When $\phi_{32} = 0$, there is no trade diversion and firms located in the first country receive all the benefits from the antidumping duty. To see why this is so, note that

$$(3.18) \quad D_{2ad} = \phi_{22} N_{2ad} + \phi_{32} N_{3ad} = 0$$

This equation links the damage suffered by firms in the third country to the amount of trade diversion received by firms in the second country. What the equation shows is that it will only be profitable for firms in the second country to enter if the third country has a foothold in the second country. This is because the antidumping duty reduces the number of third country firms exporting to the second country. This reduction makes it profitable for new second country firms to enter. But if there are no third country firms exporting to the second country, the number of varieties available in that country will not change and hence it will not be profitable for new firms to enter.[6]

The welfare effects of the antidumping duty can be computed using (3.6) in conjunction with (3.12)-(3.17)

$$(3.19) \quad W_{1ad} = B_1 \phi_{31} t_{ad} > 0$$

$$(3.20) \quad W_{2ad} = 0$$

$$(3.21) \quad W_{3ad} = - (b_3 A_3 \sigma_{31} \mu_1 t_{ad}) / \sigma_{33} < 0$$

The antidumping duty produces a gain in welfare in the first country, no change in welfare in the second country, and a loss of welfare in the third country.[7] The welfare gain experienced by the first country is due entirely to an increase in the number of varieties produced worldwide[8] and is not peculiar to this model.[9]

Consider next the effects of a safeguard on product variety and output per firm. Remember that the safeguard considered in this chapter is a simple non-discriminatory tariff. The safeguard has the following effects[10]

(3.22) $X_{1sg} = 0$

(3.23) $X_{2sg} = \sigma_{21} \mu_1 (b_2 - b_1) t_{sg} < 0$

(3.24) $X_{3sg} = \dfrac{\sigma_{22}\sigma_{31}(b_3 - b_1) + \sigma_{21}\sigma_{32}(b_2 - b_3)}{\sigma_{22}} \mu_1 t_{sg} < 0$

(3.25) $N_{1sg} = [b_3\mu_1(\sigma_{22}\sigma_{31} - \sigma_{21}\sigma_{32}) (\phi_{22}\phi_{31} - \phi_{21}\phi_{32}) +$

$b_1\sigma_{22}\sigma_{33}\phi_{22}(1 - \phi_{11}) + b_2\mu_1\sigma_{21}\sigma_{33}\phi_{21}] t_{sg} /$

$(\sigma_{21}\sigma_{32}\phi_{22}\phi_{31}) > 0$

(3.26) $N_{2sg} = \dfrac{b_3\phi_{32}(\sigma_{22}\sigma_{31} - \sigma_{21}\sigma_{32}) - \sigma_{21}\sigma_{33}b_2}{\sigma_{22}\sigma_{33}\phi_{22}} \mu_1 t_{sg} < 0$

(3.27) $N_{3sg} = \dfrac{\sigma_{32}\sigma_{21} - \sigma_{31}\sigma_{22}}{\sigma_{22}\sigma_{33}} b_3 \mu_1 t_{sg} < 0$

As expected, total output rises in the first country and declines in the second and third countries. The welfare effects of the safeguard are given by

(3.28) $W_{1sg} = B_1 (\phi_{21} + \phi_{31}) t_{sg} > 0$

$$(3.29) \quad W_{2sg} = - (b_2 \, A_2 \, \sigma_{21} \, \mu_1 \, t_{sg}) \, / \, \sigma_{22} < 0$$

$$(3.30) \quad W_{3sg} = - \frac{\sigma_{32}\sigma_{21} - \sigma_{31}\sigma_{22}}{\sigma_{22}\sigma_{33}} \, b_3 \, A_3 \, \mu_1 \, t_{sg} < 0$$

Again, welfare rises in the first country as a result of a tariff, and for exactly the same reason as before. The safeguard raises the number of varieties produced worldwide.[11] As expected, welfare declines in the second and third countries because the number of varieties consumed in these countries declines.

I begin by determining the equivalent tariff rate for the Having solved for the effects of both the antidumping duty and the safeguard, I now turn to the question of efficacy. The question of which tariff is more effective is answered by equating the welfare effects of the two tariffs and then seeing which tariff provides a greater amount of relief to the domestic industry. Remember that relief is measured by changes in the domestic industry's total output.

I begin by determining the equivalent tariff rate for the safeguard (i.e. the tariff rate which has the same effect on domestic welfare as the antidumping duty.) It is easy to see that the two tariffs will have the same effect on domestic welfare if

$$(3.31) \quad t_{sg} = [\phi_{31} \, / \, (\phi_{21} + \phi_{31})] \, t_{ad}$$

Since output per firm is constant in the first country under either tariff, the relief received by the domestic industry as a result of a particular tariff is captured by the change in the number of varieties produced in the first country. Thus the difference between the changes in product variety under the antidumping duty and the safeguard can be used as a measure of efficacy. This difference is given by

$$(3.32) \quad N_{1ad} - N_{1sg} = [b_3(\sigma_{22}\sigma_{31} - \sigma_{21}\sigma_{32}) - b_2\sigma_{21}\sigma_{33}]$$

$$[\frac{\mu_1 \, \phi_{21}}{\sigma_{22}\sigma_{33}\phi_{11}\phi_{22}}] \, t_{sg}$$

In the absence of retaliation, the safeguard is always superior to the antidumping duty when trade diversion is present (i.e. when ϕ_{32} is non-zero.) The proof that (3.32) is negative under these circumstances is given in Appendix D. In the absence of both foreign retaliation and trade diversion, however, (3.32) may be positive. This is not a particularly surprising result because it is the trade diversion which undermines the efficacy of antidumping duties. Without trade diversion, antidumping duties are more effective and hence more likely to be superior to non-discriminatory safeguards. A proof of this result is provided in Appendix D.

In the remainder of the chapter, I consider only the case in which trade diversion is present (i.e. $\phi_{32} > 0$.) Even in this case, it is still possible that an antidumping duty will be superior to a safeguard. This possibility arises because safeguards usually involve some retaliation by foreign governments. The remainder of this section analyzes the effects of this retaliation on the efficacy of antidumping duties.

The safeguard imposes two costs on the second and third countries. The first is the welfare loss suffered by its consumers, who will consume fewer varieties. The second is the contraction of the industries in the second and third countries. For simplicity, suppose the foreign governments place no weight on the welfare loss suffered by their consumers and seek compensation only for the loss suffered by their industries. If the antidumping duty is superior to the safeguard under this limited definition of retaliation, it will remain superior under broader definitions.

To incorporate retaliation into the model, I first determine the value that each government attaches to the changes brought about by the antidumping duty and the safeguard. Let $V_i(N_iX_i)$ give the value to the ith government of an industry with aggregate output N_iX_i. For simplicity, assume that

(3.33) $V_i(N_iX_i) = k N_iX_i$ $k > 0$

so that the value that a government attaches to its own industry is directly proportional to the total output of that industry. This assumption is justified on two grounds: first, there are no profits in this model; second, increases in total output will reflect increases in the industry's employment and international market share.

Because (3.32) is negative, the increase in the first country's total output under the safeguard is greater than the increase in its aggregate output under the antidumping duty if there is no retaliation. This implies that

(3.34) $V_{1sg} > V_{1ad}$

where V_{1sg} and V_{1ad} are the changes in the value of the first industry under the safeguard and the antidumping duty respectively. The question now is whether the safeguard is still superior to the antidumping duty after the costs of retaliation are accounted for.

The safeguard will be superior to the antidumping duty if and only if

$$(3.35) \quad \sum_{i=1}^{3} V_i V_{isg} > V_1 V_{1ad}$$

The term on the left hand side represents the net change in value for the first government after the costs of retaliation are accounted for. The costs of retaliation represent the compensation that the second and third countries would have to receive for them to be indifferent between the safeguard and free trade.

From (3.35), it is clear that the initial values of all three industries are important in determining which tariff is more effective. Since the value of an industry is proportional to its size, the greater is the size of the domestic industry relative to the size of the foreign industries, the more effective is the safeguard. The intuition behind this result is obvious: the greater is the size of the domestic industry relative to the size of the foreign industries, the greater are the benefits from the safeguard relative to the compensation.

To control for these differences in size, assume that all three industries have the same initial value. From (3.33), I know that this assumption implies that all three industries have the same initial output. Combining this assumption with (3.35), I find that the safeguard will now be more effective than the antidumping duty if and only if

$$(3.36) \quad \sum_{i=1}^{3} (N_{isg} + X_{isg}) > N_{1ad} + X_{1ad}$$

Further substitution yields the following necessary and sufficient condition which insures that the safeguard is superior to the antidumping duty

$$(3.37) \quad \{ \frac{\phi_{21} - \phi_{11}}{\phi_{11}\phi_{22}} [b_3(\sigma_{21}\sigma_{32} - \sigma_{22}\sigma_{31}) + b_2\sigma_{21}\sigma_{33}] \} +$$

$$\sigma_{33}[\sigma_{22}(\sigma_{21} + \sigma_{31})(b_2 - b_1) + (\sigma_{22}\sigma_{31} - \sigma_{21}\sigma_{32})(b_2 - b_3)]$$

$$- 2b_3(\sigma_{22}\sigma_{31} - \sigma_{21}\sigma_{32}) > 0$$

This condition will never hold if ϕ_{21} is less than ϕ_{11}, something which is always true if all three industries have the same initial output. Thus when we control for the size of the industries, the antidumping duty will always be superior to the safeguard when retaliation occurs.

It should be emphasized that the welfare loss of consumers in the second and third countries has been ignored. If we include this loss, the amount of compensation will be greater, making the safeguard even less effective. Thus antidumping duty are likely to be superior to safeguards under more general conditions if the safeguards trigger retaliation.

3.6 Conclusion

In recent years, discriminatory policies designed to deal with unfair trade practices have been invoked with increasing frequency while more traditional non-discriminatory trade policies such as safeguards have fallen out of vogue. This pattern has arisen even though discriminatory trade policies are usually viewed as less effective because of the trade diversion which accompanies them. The explanation for this pattern offered here is that non-discriminatory policies frequently involve the possibility of legally sanctioned retaliation, and this raises the costs associated with them. This explanation is consistent with the fact that several different U.S. presidents have rejected safeguards even when the imports involved have clearly damaged U.S. industries. Many of the same U.S. industries which have unsuccessfully sought relief through safeguards have been successful in obtaining relief through antidumping duties. The model developed in this chapter indicates that the reason for this success is that the U.S. government finds it less costly to offer protection through legally sanctioned discriminatory trade policies (such as antidumping duties) than through retaliation prone non-discriminatory policies such as safeguards.

NOTES

1. The tariff could also be viewed as the tariff equivalent of a quota.

2. For a proof, see Helpman and Krugman, Chapter 6.

3. Log differentiating the demand function and simplifying, we find that the first country's price elasticity of demand for any of the varieties produced in i can be expressed as

$$(b_1 + 1) - [b_1 P_{i1}^{-b_1} / (\sum_{k=1}^{3} N_k P_{k1}^{-b_1})]$$

The last term in this expression is of the order $1/J$ where $J = N_1 + N_2 + N_3$. I will assume that J is large, so that the last term is negligible.

4. See Helpman [1984], pg. 358.

5. See Appendix B for proof that $\phi_{31} \phi_{22} - \phi_{21} \phi_{32} > 0$.

6. One has to be careful in interpreting this last result. It does not imply that it is unprofitable for new firms in the second country to enter the first country's market but rather that it is

unprofitable for them to enter both their home and export markets. This last point raises the question of foreign investment. Firms entering from both the second and third countries will have an incentive (higher profits) to locate in the first country. I have chosen to ignore this question because it is difficult to define trade diversion in this case. In fact, this kind of relocation has become a problem in the EC, which has recently adopted "screwdriver" laws to prevent foreign firms from avoiding antidumping duties. For a further discussion, see Webb [1987].

7. The first country's welfare gain may still arise even if the optimal MFN tariff is initially in place, although this is not a necessary result. This is because the optimal MFN tariff is optimal only in the sense that it is an optimal non-discriminatory tariff. If we allow for discriminatory tariffs, such as antidumping duties, it cannot be the case that the optimal MFN tariff is superior to the optimal combination of discriminatory tariffs.

8. See Appendix C for a proof of this result.

9. See Lancaster [1984] or Flam and Helpman [1987] for some other examples.

10. See Appendix B for proof that $\sigma_{22}\sigma_{31} - \sigma_{21}\sigma_{32} > 0$.

11. See Appendix C for a proof.

Chapter 4: An Empirical Model of Efficacy

4.1 Introduction

In this chapter, I simulate the effects that an antidumping duty and a non-discriminatory safeguard have on an American industry and its foreign competitors. The goal of the chapter is to assess the efficacy of two antidumping duties levied by the U.S. in 1983 and 1984. Efficacy is determined by comparing the effects of the antidumping duties with two hypothetical non-discriminatory tariffs, which represent safeguards. The more effective tariff will be the one which provides a given amount of relief to a domestic industry at the lowest cost to U.S. consumers.

Safeguards were chosen for comparative purposes because they represent a natural alternative to antidumping duties. Norall [1987] and Finger and Murray [1990] argue that antidumping duties have in large part become a substitute for safeguards. This is because the conditions for obtaining relief under antidumping laws are weaker than those for safeguards and because retaliation is not sanctioned when antidumping duties are imposed. Under the GATT, exporting countries adversely affected by safeguards have a legal right to retaliate.

Why should trade economists be concerned with the efficacy of antidumping duties? Some insight is obtained by noting that the original intent of antidumping duties was to end predatory pricing by foreign firms. The motivation for antidumping duties in this context is clear: they serve to maintain competition. Unfortunately, few U.S. antidumping cases have involved predatory pricing. In practice, antidumping duties have served primarily to limit competition by restricting the prices foreign firms can charge. Whether or not predatory pricing is present has become irrelevant.

When viewed in this way, the efficacy of antidumping duties becomes important because there may be alternatives to antidumping duties which can provide the same amount of relief to domestic firms but at a lower cost to domestic consumers. Measuring the amount of relief provided by an antidumping duty as well as the associated welfare costs will be the first step in determining whether these duties are an effective way of providing relief to domestic firms. The second step will be to determine the welfare costs associated with an equivalent safeguard. By comparing the welfare losses generated by the two tariffs, we can then determine which tariff is more effective.

Several other authors have tried to assess the efficacy of antidumping duties. Most notably, Messerlin [1988] examined the antidumping cases brought before the European Community between 1980 and 1985. The methodology employed by Messerlin amounted to comparing trade flows before and after the antidumping investigations. Changes in these trade flows were used to measure of the impact of antidumping duties. Messerlin concluded that the EC antidumping regulations "have a strong protectionist content and represent a threat to the GATT edifice."

While Messerlin's methodology allows him to make generalize across a large number of antidumping cases, it suffers from an obvious weakness in that it implicitly assumes that other conditions remain constant during the sample period. Changes in these conditions during the sample period can produce seriously misleading results. For example, changes in trade policy following the initiation or completion of an antidumping case may give the impression that antidumping duties are providing more or less protection than they really are. Without controlling for such changes, it is difficult to know what impact antidumping duties have.

Another significant study of the efficacy of antidumping duties was conducted by Eichengreen and van der Ven [1984]. They constructed and calibrated an oligopolistic model of the steel industry in order to measure the impact of the Trigger Price Mechanism (TPM), a program instituted by the Treasury Department in the late seventies to monitor the dumping of steel imports. Their results, as they readily admit, are at best suggestive and vary widely depending on the choice of parameters.

The methodology that I employ in this chapter involves estimating a system of equations and then using the parameter estimates to conduct simulations. In particular, I simulate the paths of prices, output, profits and welfare with and without an antidumping duty in place, and with a safeguard in place. The efficacy of the antidumping duty is then determined by comparing the paths of the endogenous variables under the different tariff regimes.

The principal strengths of this approach are that the ceteris paribus assumption of Messerlin and the calibrations of Eichengreen and van der Ven are no longer necessary. The main weakness of the method is that I must gather a large amount of highly disaggregated data for each case. In many cases, the data is either unavailable or of poor quality, making a general study of efficacy similar to Messerlin's impossible. Even if all the data were available, the cost of estimating a system of equations for each case would be prohibitive. Thus the methodology adopted here should be viewed as a complement to the work of Messerlin and Eichengreen and van der Ven.

Grossman [1986] uses a similar methodology in his study of the effects of import competition on the domestic steel industry. My approach differs from his in several respects. First, Grossman analyzes changes in total imports while I examine changes in imports from particular countries or groups of countries. I do this because I am interested in determining the extent of any trade diversion generated by the antidumping duties and hence I must look at disaggregated imports. A second difference is that Grossman uses functional forms which are log linear, and this allows him to derive and estimate reduced forms. I use a much more general non-linear system of preferences and thus I cannot derive reduced forms. This makes the simulation task more difficult, since feedback effects must now be considered. Incorporating these feedback effects into the analysis requires finding the roots of a system of non-linear equations. Finally, I consider a single product rather than an entire industry, as Grossman does. This allows me to make certain assumptions which cannot be justified at the industry level.

The remainder of this chapter is divided into 6 sections. The first section provides background information on the two products involved in the analysis. In the second and third sections, I describe preferences and production. In the fourth section, I describe the data employed and give its sources. The fifth section presents the parameter estimates and the simulation results. The final section summarizes the results of the chapter.

4.2 A Description of the Products Involved

Both the case studies I will conduct involve products produced by the U.S. steel industry: the first product is stainless steel sheet and strip and the second product is carbon steel plate. I chose these two products because they have both been the target of antidumping duties and because data was available for both of them. Antidumping duties were levied against French and West German imports of sheet and strip in July, 1983 and against Brazilian imports of plate in March, 1984. Another reason for selecting these two products is that steel products have been involved in a large number of antidumping cases. If the two cases considered here are representative of the other antidumping cases involving steel products, the results will have broader implications.

I now briefly describe each of the products and provide some background information which will prove useful later in the chapter.

4.2.1 Stainless Steel Sheet and Strip

Stainless steel is an alloy steel containing, by weight, not less than 11.5% chromium and not more than 1% carbon. Stainless steel sheet is used in food processing and hospital equipment, in liquid gas storage tanks and in defense materials. Stainless steel strip is used in the production of cars, appliances and industrial equipment. In the last ten years, sheet and strip have been produced in the U.S. by 15 firms, with 4 of these firms accounting for the majority of production.

The production of stainless steel takes place in an electric furnace. Steel scrap is combined with chromium and other alloys such as nickel and molybdenum in an electric furnace to produce molten steel. The molten steel is continuously cast and hot-rolled to produce coil. After the coil is annealed and descaled, it is then cold-rolled and further processed to produce sheet and strip.

I assume that the production of sheet and strip involves only four variable inputs: steel scrap, labor, electricity and chromium. Chromium is the most important alloying element in stainless steel; inputs of the other alloying elements vary significantly across grades and were thus excluded. I assume that the electric furnace is a fixed input because the sample period is less than four years. This is a short time to adjust capacity through the construction of new plants.

Since 1980, imported stainless steel products have been the target of many U.S. trade restrictions. In December of 1981, allegations of unfair trade practices were made against several stainless steel importers, but these allegations were dropped in favor of an escape clause action in November of 1982. In May of 1983, the International Trade Commission ruled in the affirmative on this escape clause action and the President granted relief in July of 1983. The relief took the form of increased duties on imports of stainless steel plate, sheet and strip, and quotas on the remaining stainless steel products. Relief was granted for a four year period, during which time the duties and quotas would be phased out.

In July of 1983, antidumping duties were levied against French and German imports of sheet and strip. The duties levied were relatively small, being roughly equal to 5% in both cases. At that time, French and German imports accounted for about 25% of total sheet and strip imports. In September of 1984, the President established a national policy for the steel industry which eventually produced voluntary export restraints on imports of most steel mill products, including stainless steel sheet and strip. The restraints on stainless steel sheet and strip did not go into effect until March of 1986. Both the antidumping duties were terminated at this point.

Table 4-1 presents data on U.S. shipments, consumption, and imports of stainless steel sheet and strip between 1980 and 1986. A glance at this table shows that increased imports seriously eroded U.S. market share between 1980 and 1986.

Table 4-1: Shipments, consumption and imports of stainless steel sheet and strip (in thousands of short tons)

	1980	1981	1982	1983	1984	1985	1986
1 Domestic shipments	617	715	565	711	739	777	688
2 Apparent consump.	655	787	652	794	876	911	839
3 Capacity util. (%)	59	61	46	76	84	85	71
4 Imports	38	72	87	83	137	135	151
5 Ratio of 4 to 1	0.06	0.10	0.15	0.12	0.18	0.17	0.22
6 Ratio of 4 to 2	0.06	0.09	0.13	0.10	0.16	0.15	0.18

Source: *Quarterly Report on Specialty Steel Products*

The market share of imports tripled from 1980 to 1986. As we might expect, two of the most notable increases took place in 1981 and 1982, years in which U.S. sheet and strip producers faced unrestricted import competition. In 1983, the imposition of tariffs and antidumping duties had a negative impact on imports, both in absolute and relative terms. Imports surged in 1984, registering an increase of 75% despite the presence of additional tariffs. This increase is probably explained more by the booming demand for sheet and strip than by any loss in U.S. competitiveness. Apparent consumption rose to a 5 year high in 1984 while U.S. firms operated at nearly 84% of capacity, also a five year high. A similar story can be told in 1985 and 1986.

4.2.2 Carbon Steel Plate

Carbon steel plate is a finished steel mill product used in industries such as non-electric machinery, non-residential construction and shipbuilding. About 15 firms produce carbon steel plate domestically, with 4 of these firms accounting for roughly 70% of domestic production. While there are several types of carbon steel plate, this chapter focuses on hot-rolled plate, which accounted for roughly 75% of total domestic plate production over the sample period.

The production of carbon steel plate takes place in integrated steel mills. In these mills, coal, iron ore and limestone are combined in a blast furnace to produce molten iron. The molten iron is mixed with steel scrap and other inputs and placed in a furnace (either open hearth, basic oxygen or electric.) The product of this mix is molten steel, which is cast into semifinished shapes using either continuous casting or conventional ingot casting. These semifinished shapes are rolled or otherwise processed into a myriad of finished steel mill products, including carbon steel plate.

Rather than try to model the entire process described above, I will model only the finishing process. This allows me to simplify the supply side of the model by collapsing many of the primary inputs, such as coal, limestone, and iron ore, into a single intermediate input, raw steel. This raw steel is combined with labor and energy in a rolling mill to produce carbon steel plate. Following Grossman, I assume that the capital stock grows at an exogenously determined rate. Unlike Grossman, I allow firms to select the fraction of the capital stock employed in any one period. Thus firms are free to choose the level of capacity utilization.

Since 1978, several restrictions have affected imports of carbon steel plate. The first restriction involved the Trigger Price Mechanism (TPM), which went into effect in 1978. The TPM was designed to stop the dumping of imported steel products below certain prices. It provided for the monitoring of import prices by the U.S. government and the self initiation of dumping investigations in cases in which dumping occurred. The TPM was suspended in January of 1980, revamped, and reinstituted in September of that year. It was suspended again and largely discarded in January of 1982. In the fall of 1982, the U.S. reached an agreement with the EC in which the EC voluntarily restrained its exports of carbon steel plate and other steel products.

Table 4-2: Shipments, consumption and imports of carbon steel plate (in thousands of short tons)

	1978	1979	1980	1981	1982	1983	1984
1 Domestic shipments	6136	6651	6113	5810	3038	2802	3110
2 Apparent consump.	8452	7886	7651	7497	4106	3766	4453
3 Capacity util. (%)	64	64	62	56	29	27	NA
4 Imports	2150	1252	1571	1841	1152	1028	1406
5 Ratio of 4 to 1	0.30	0.18	0.25	0.32	0.38	0.37	0.45
6 Ratio of 4 to 2	0.23	0.16	0.20	0.25	0.28	0.27	0.32

Source: *Monthly Report on Selected Steel Industry Data*

In April of 1984, the U.S. levied an 80% antidumping duty against Brazilian imports of carbon steel plate. The duty was terminated in December of 1984, when the President's national steel policy went into effect. The President's steel program replaced the antidumping duty with a voluntary export restraint.

Table 4-2 provides data on U.S. shipments, consumption, and imports of carbon steel plate between 1978 and 1984. During this period, the ratio of plate imports to apparent consumption increased nearly 35% while U.S. production fell by 50%. The surge in imports and the poor health of U.S. plate producers help to explain why import relief was granted during this period.

4.3 Preferences

In this section, I describe the demand for stainless steel sheet and strip and the demand for carbon steel plate. The key assumption is that each product is differentiated rather than homogeneous. Evidence of product differentiation in the steel industry takes the form of significantly lower prices for virtually all imported steel products. If steel were a homogeneous product, we would not observe such a sustained price differential; U.S. producers would either have to cut prices or be driven out of business. But even though imported steel has underpriced U.S. steel for over twenty years, imports account for only about 20% of the U.S. market. This is a sign that steel products are differentiated.

What is the basis of product differentiation in the steel industry? Jondrow, Chase and Gamble [1982] conduct a study of the factors which serve to differentiate imported and domestic steel. Their results suggest that imported steel is differentiated from domestic steel in several ways, the two most important being differences in lead times and differences in security of supply. The authors calculate that these two factors alone may account for a price differential of 18%. Crandall [1981] also finds that imported and domestic steel are differentiated. He argues that "the U.S. steel market consists of two types of buyers: those desiring long term arrangements with secure domestic suppliers and those more interested in minimizing their short term cost of steel."

Since imported and domestic steel are differentiated, it is reasonable to assume that imported steel is differentiated as well. I assume that imported steel is differentiated by its country of origin (see Armington [1969] for a discussion.) Using this assumption, the demand for steel products produced in country i is assumed to take the form[1]

$$(4.1) \quad X_i = \frac{a_i \, b_i \, Y^{b_i} \, [P_i \, (1 + t_i)]^{-(b_i+1)}}{\sum_{j=1}^{n} a_j \, b_j \, Y^{b_j-1} \, [P_j \, (1 + t_j)]^{-b_j}}$$

where X_i is the U.S. demand for output produced in country i, P_i is the price of output sold in the U.S. and produced in country i, and t_i is the tariff levied by the U.S. on output produced in country i. The variable Y represents a measure of U.S. industrial activity, which is an indicator of the position of the demand curve. The parameter n represents the number of countries supplying the particular steel product to the American market. It can be shown[2] that b_i is about equal to the elasticity of demand for output produced in country i. I chose the preferences embodied in (4.1) because they allow for a very general pattern of substitutability between varieties produced in different countries. It is easy to show that if $b_i = b_j$ for all i and j, then preferences will be of the CES type.

Following Varian [1978], I will not estimate (4.1) for all n countries. Instead, take the log of the ratio of X_i to X_j for all i not equal to j. This yields n-1 equations of the form

$$(4.2) \quad \ln(X_i/X_j) = \ln(a_i b_i/a_j b_j) + (b_i - b_j)\ln Y +$$

$$(b_j + 1)\ln[P_j (1 + t_j) - (b_i + 1) \ln[P_i (1 + t_i)]$$

I estimate the n-1 equations in (4.2) for every case except the one in which i equals j. In that case, I estimated (4.1) directly. Notice that parametric restrictions must be imposed both within and across the n equations contained in (4.1) and (4.2)

The demand functions discussed above are derived from the following indirect utility function

$$(4.3) \quad V_{US} = \sum_{j=1}^{n} a_j Y^{b_j} [P_j (1 + t_j)]^{-b_j}$$

where V_{US} is the indirect utility of a representative agent in the U.S. The welfare loss experienced by consumers as a result of the antidumping duty or the safeguard is estimated by looking at how (4.3) changes when the various tariffs are introduced.

4.4 Production

Assume that the production function of a representative firm is of the form

$$(4.4) \quad X_{us} = \min (c_1 z_1, \ldots, c_m z_m)$$

where X_{US} is the domestic firm's total output, c_i is the ith input-output coefficient and z_i is the quantity of the ith input. Equation (4.4) is a fixed coefficients Leontief technology. I chose this technology because it reflects the limited input substitution available in both production processes. In principle, it will be easier to work with the cost function associated with (4.4). This is because the cost function is only a function of total output and factor prices. The cost function associated with the simple Leontief technology is given by

$$(4.5) \quad C_{us}(\mathbf{W}, X_{us}) = X_{us}^{1/\delta} \left[\sum_{i=1}^{m} \phi_i W_i \right]$$

where W_i is the price of the ith input, $\mathbf{W}$ is the vector of these input prices, and δ is a scale parameter.[3]

Implicit in equation (4.5) is the assumption that factor prices are exogenously determined. This assumption is justified because all of the inputs in the production process outlined above are used extensively through out the steel or stainless steel industries. Changes in the demand for these inputs by plate or sheet and strip producers are not likely to influence factor prices because carbon steel plate and stainless steel sheet and strip represent only a small fraction of the industry's total output of steel products.

Given the technology specified in (4.4) and (4.5), U.S. firms maximize profits by solving

$$(4.6) \quad \underset{X_{us}}{\text{Max}} \quad P_{us} X_{us} - C_{us}(\mathbf{W}, X_{us})$$

I assume that U.S. firms behave as monopolistic competitors vis-a-vis the rest of the world, and as a result, they follow a simple mark up rule when setting prices. Solving for this mark up rule and taking logs yields

$$(4.7) \quad \ln P_{us} = \mu_1 + \mu_2 \ln X_{us} + \ln(\sum_{i=1}^{m} \phi_i W_i)$$

where $\mu_1 = \ln[(b_{us}+1)/(b_{us} \delta)]$

$\mu_2 = (1-\delta)/\delta$

I assume that the prices of imported plate and imported sheet and strip are exogenously determined. This assumption is justified in part by Grossman, who tested the hypothesis that the overall supply of imported steel was perfectly elastic between 1973 and 1983. He could not reject this hypothesis at the 85% level of significance. This finding is consistent with the widely held view that the world steel market was characterized by considerable excess capacity during the late seventies and early eighties.

4.5 The Data

For the case involving stainless steel sheet and strip, monthly observations were drawn from the period beginning in October of 1982 and ending in February of 1986. I chose this period because monthly data on U.S. production of sheet and strip were not available before this date and because the U.S. imposed quotas in February of 1986. For the case involving carbon steel plate, monthly observations were drawn from the period beginning in July of 1978 and ending in December of 1984. I selected this period for two reasons. First, Brazil began exporting plate to the U.S. in earnest in July of 1978. Second, the SIP imposed quotas on imports of plate from many countries in December of 1984.

In the case involving sheet and strip, imports from France and West Germany were considered separately while imports from the rest of the world were combined into a single group. In the case involving plate, imports from Belgium, Brazil, Canada, Japan, South Korea, Spain and West Germany were considered separately. These seven countries were responsible for 70% of U.S. plate imports over the sample period. Many other countries which export plate to the U.S. could not be included because their exports and unit values were not consistently available over the sample period.

Data on the domestic production of sheet and strip were obtained from the *Quarterly Report on Specialty Steel Products*. The output data includes all grades of sheet and strip. A proxy for the domestic price of sheet and strip was also obtained from the same source. A proxy for the domestic price of sheet and strip was used because prices for all grades of sheet and strip were not available. The proxy is the price of cold-rolled stainless steel sheet. The grade is AISI number 304, and this grade represents the majority of the sheet sold in the U.S. While strip prices were not available, the similarities between sheet and strip in both production and grade mix makes the price of cold-rolled sheet a good proxy for the price of strip.

Data on the domestic production of plate were obtained from the *Survey of Current Business* (1978-81) and from the *Monthly Report on Selected Steel Industry Data* (1982-84). List prices for domestic plate were taken from *Metal Statistics*. Unfortunately, list prices are of little value in the steel industry, where discounting is common place. To allow for this discounting and for the provision of extras (such as cutting to particular specifications), annual realized prices for plate from the Commerce Department's publication *Current Industrial Reports: Steel Mill Products* were combined with list prices to construct annual discount factors. These annual discount factors were multiplied by the monthly list prices in each year to obtain estimates of the discounted monthly prices.

The weekly earnings of blast furnace workers were taken from the BLS publication *Employment and Earnings*. While these wages do not represent the wages of workers employed in the production of stainless steel or in the finishing of carbon steel, they were the best alternative. The prices of electricity, natural gas and residual fuels were taken from the BLS publication *Producer Prices and Price Indexes*. The energy variable is a weighted average of the costs of electricity, natural gas and residual fuels, where the weights are calculated as in Duke et al [1977]. The weights are computed annually, and changes in the weights represent variations in the energy mix. Unfortunately, the weights use figures for the entire steel making process rather than just the finishing process and are biased as a result. A proxy for the cost of capital is the producer price index for machinery and equipment, which is reported in the *Survey of Current Business*. The price of chromium was taken from the Department of the Interior's publication *Mineral Industry Surveys: Chromium*.

Scrap prices were taken from the *American Metal Market*. The price of raw steel is not available, and so the price of billets was used as a proxy. Billets are a semifinished steel product, and the list price of billets was taken from *Metal Statistics* and adjusted for discounting using the same technique described above for plate.

Import volumes and unit values for sheet and strip were obtained from *U.S. General Imports: Schedule A*. Import volumes and unit values for plate were taken from *U.S. General Imports: Schedule A* (1978-81) and from *The Monthly Report on Selected Steel Industry Data* (1982-84). All unit values were initially taken at customs and then adjusted for any tariffs as well as for the cost of insurance and freight. Tarr [1979] argues that unit values provide a good approximation of export prices (given a lag of one quarter) and that the use of unit values maintains comparability which would otherwise be lost.

Unfortunately, unit values for plate imports from Brazil and Spain were not available in several months because U.S. imports from these countries were negligible during these months. For Brazil, no unit values were available during the period following the imposition of the antidumping duty in March of 1984. For this period, the annual unit value of Canadian imports from Brazil was used as a proxy. Canadian unit values are probably representative of U.S. unit values given the similarities between the two economies, but because the Canadian unit value is provided annually, it is at best a good approximation. The Canadian unit value was taken from the U.N. publication *World Trade Annual*.

The missing Spanish unit values were concentrated in the year 1983. Fortunately, quarterly Spanish home prices of plate were available in the *Metal Bulletin* for the entire sample period. Interpolating this quarterly data yielded a monthly series of Spanish home prices. Regressing the available Spanish unit values on this monthly series produced an equation used to estimate the missing unit values.[4]

Tariff rates and antidumping duties were taken from the *Federal Register* and *Tariff Schedules of the U.S.: Annotated*. The cost of insurance and freight was taken from *U.S. General Imports: Schedule A*. The indexes of industrial production for durable manufactures and for non-electric machinery are used as measures of industrial activity for sheet/strip and plate, respectively. Both indexes were obtained from the *Survey of Current Business*. Finally, all prices were deflated by the producer price index, which was obtained from *Producer Prices and Price Indexes*.

4.6 The Results

For each case, equations (4.1), (4.2), and (4.7) are estimated simultaneously using iterative non-linear three stage least squares (N3SLS). Amemiya [1985] and others have shown that the N3SLS estimates are consistent if the errors from each equation are i.i.d. and if the overall error vector has a zero mean with covariance matrix Σ. This is not true for the principal alternative technique, full information maximum likelihood (FIML). FIML will produce an asymptotically smaller covariance matrix then N3SLS if the error terms are normally distributed. But if the normality assumption is incorrect, FIML will not produce consistent estimates. Since there is no reason to believe that the error terms here have a normal distribution, N3SLS is the more attractive technique.

I compute the N3SLS estimates by minimizing the following generalized sum of squares

$$(4.9) \quad [r' \, (S^{-1} \otimes W) \, r] \, / \, n$$

where n is the number of observations on each dependent variable, r is the ngx1 vector of stacked residuals from the g equations, S is a gxg estimate of Σ, W is an nxn projection matrix for the instrumental variables (see Gallant and Jorgenson [1979] for more detail) and $\otimes$ is the symbol for Kronecker product. I use all the exogenous variables of the system as instruments. The method used to compute the estimates is the Marquardt-Levenberg method (see Amemiya for more detail.)

The technique is iterative in the sense that both the estimates and the estimated covariance matrix must converge. The initial estimate of the covariance matrix are obtained via non-linear two stage least squares. Using this S matrix, the N3SLS estimates are computed and checked for convergence. If the estimates have not converged, the procedure computes a new set of estimates using the same S matrix and the previous estimates. If the estimates have converged, the S matrix is checked for convergence as follows. A new S matrix is formed using the converged parameter estimates; this matrix is then compared with the previous S matrix. If the S matrix has converged, the procedure stops; otherwise, the new S matrix is used to compute another set of estimates and the procedure begins anew.

The standard errors of the parameter estimates are based on the assumption that the distribution of the parameter estimates is normal. While this assumption will hold asymptotically, the small sample properties of the estimates are unknown. Thus it is likely that the standard errors reported here are smaller than the true standard errors.

I compute the effects of the antidumping duty by using the parameter estimates derived above to conduct simulations. I conduct the simulations as follows. First, the roots of the non-linear system consisting of equations (4.1), (4.2) and (4.7) are obtained. These roots represent the values of the endogenous variables which satisfy the parameterized versions of equations (4.1), (4.2) and (4.7) in each period. The technique used to find these roots is the Newton method. The solution technique is dynamic because the roots are obtained period by period. Thus any lagged endogenous variables take on the values of the roots in the previous period.

Having obtained these roots, I then remove the antidumping duty and repeat the process. The new set of roots represent the simulated values of the endogenous variables in the absence of the antidumping duty. I compute the effects of the antidumping duty by comparing the two different sets of roots.

In addition to computing the effects of the antidumping duties, I also simulate the impact of two equivalent safeguards using the same procedure. The most important reason for doing this is to determine whether these tariffs can provide the same amount of relief to the domestic industry at a lower cost to domestic consumers. Each safeguard is equivalent to the respective antidumping duty in that they provide the same amount of relief to the domestic industry in each period. In order to equate the effects of the antidumping duty and the safeguard in each period, it was necessary to vary the safeguard from period to period. While this is not realistic, there was no real alternative since no single tariff rate can provide the same amount of protection to the domestic industry in each period.

I compute the equivalent safeguard in each period as follows. First, in each period, I fix U.S. output and prices at the level generated by the antidumping duty. Second, I replace the known antidumping duty with the unknown safeguard. Finally, I compute the roots of the new system for each period. One of these roots represents the tariff rate associated with the safeguard in that period. I then use the tariff rate to calculate the welfare loss resulting from the imposition of the safeguard.

Having described the estimation and simulation procedures, consider next the results. I discuss the results from the sheet and strip case first.

4.6.1 Results from the Sheet and Strip Case

The estimation results from the case involving stainless steel sheet and strip are given in Tables 4-3 and 4-4. The parameter estimates are given in Table 4-3 while Table 4-4 provides summary statistics for each equation. Examining the parameter estimates first, note that the German and the rest of the world (ROW) demand elasticities are highly significant while the U.S. and French demand elasticities are only marginally significant. While all the demand elasticities have the correct sign, it is somewhat surprising to see that the French elasticity is smaller than the U.S. elasticity, even if both parameters are only marginally significant. Given the presence of product differentiation, the U.S. elasticity of demand should be lower than

Table 4-3: Parameter estimates for stainless steel sheet and strip

Parameter	Estimate	Standard error	T-statistic
Constants			
$a_{fre,usa}$	-3.75	1.85	-2.02
$a_{ger,usa}$	-2.15	1.94	-1.11
$a_{row,usa}$	0.81	1.95	0.41
Demand elasticities			
$b_{fre} + 1$	1.53	1.10	1.39
$b_{ger} + 1$	3.07	0.47	6.48
$b_{row} + 1$	3.29	0.76	4.35
$b_{usa} + 1$	2.00	1.15	1.74
Technological parameters			
δ	1.06	0.11	9.90
ϕ_{labor}	5.06	7.85	0.65
ϕ_{scrap}	1.54	1.87	0.82
ϕ_{elect}	0.16	0.81	0.20
ϕ_{chrom}	1.42	1.77	0.80

Table 4-4: Equation results for stainless steel sheet and strip

Dependent variable	Mean	Root MSE	D.W. statistic
$\ln(X_{fre}/X_{usa})$	-3.41	0.75	2.17
$\ln(X_{ger}/X_{usa})$	-4.86	0.84	2.21
$\ln(X_{row}/X_{usa})$	-2.17	0.33	2.47
$\ln(X_{usa})$	10.96	0.13	1.53
$\ln(P_{usa})$	7.36	0.03	1.74

the elasticity of demand for imports because U.S. steel has the advantages of shorter lead times and greater security of supply.

An examination of the technological parameters reveals that only the scale parameter is significant. While this parameter is slightly greater than one, the difference is not statistically significant at the 10% level, indicating that production in this case involves constant returns to scale. While all the remaining parameters are positive, none of them are statistically significant. Using a procedure recommended by Belsley, Kuh, and Welsch [1980], multicollinearity was found to affect the standard errors of these parameters, something which is not surprising given the small number of observations (40).

A summary of the results for each equation is provided in Table 4-4. The equations for U.S. price and output perform well. These equations are characterized by low root mean square errors (MSE's). On the other hand, the import equations perform poorly. This is in largely due to the volatility of unit values. Confirmation of this can be seen in the performance of the import demand equation for the ROW, which performs somewhat better than the other two import demand equations. This is probably because imports for the ROW are aggregated over many countries. As a result, the unit values for the ROW are less volatile. All of the equations were corrected for first order serial correlation.

The simulation results are given in Table 4-5. Before discussing these results, remember that the antidumping duties levied against French and German imports were in place for roughly three years and were levied at a rate of about 5%. During the observation period, French and German imports accounted for roughly 25% of total imports. Examination of the first two columns in Table 4-5 indicates that the overall effects of the two antidumping duties were small. French imports fall by about 4% while German imports decline by about 15%. The difference can be attributed to the greater elasticity of demand facing German imports and to the slightly higher antidumping duties levied against German imports.

As expected, imports from the ROW rose, but only slightly, suggesting that trade diversion was not significant. Indeed, the increase in U.S. output was nearly ten times as great as the increase in imports from the ROW, yet even this increase represented a gain of less than one quarter of one percent of total U.S. output. Apparent consumption of sheet and strip fell by a small amount as a result of the antidumping duties while U.S. prices were virtually unchanged. U.S. profits rose slightly while U.S. welfare declined by a small amount (at least in percentage terms.)

The second two columns of Table 4-5 give the simulation results for the equivalent safeguard. Note first that the tariff associated with the non-discriminatory safeguard was levied at an average rate of 0.5%. The small size of this tariff explains the much smaller reductions in French and German imports. Because imports from the ROW have a high elasticity of demand, even this small tariff produces a relatively large decline in ROW imports. Notice also that the reduction in apparent consumption is smaller. Perhaps most significantly, the welfare loss under the safeguard is almost half that under the antidumping duty, a clear sign that the antidumping duty is an ineffective means of providing relief in this case.

Table 4-5: Simulation results for stainless steel sheet and strip

| Variable | Antidumping duty | | Safeguard | |
	Absolute change	% change	Absolute change	% change
Imports and domestic output (in short tons)				
1. French imports	-1352	-4.00	-196	-0.60
2. German imports	-1636	-14.70	-179	-1.60
3. ROW imports	217	0.20	-1971	-1.40
4. U.S. output	2079	0.20	2079	0.20
5. Apparent consumption	-692	-0.10	-266	-0.02
Prices, profits (both in 1984 dollars) and welfare				
6. U.S. prices (average change)	-0.14	0.01	-0.14	0.01
7. U.S. profits (in millions of dollars)	1.52	0.20	1.52	0.20
8. Welfare	-	-0.15	-	-0.09

4.6.2 Results from the Plate Case

Unfortunately, the parameter estimates did not converge for the carbon steel plate model. The Belgian demand elasticity did not converge in the most general model, but the model did converge after this parameter was restricted to equal the Canadian demand elasticity. This restriction is reasonable in that both Belgium and Canada have a similar share of U.S. imports over the sample period and both are developed countries with established carbon steel plate producers.

The estimation results are given in Tables 4-6 and 4-7. Table 4-6 contains the parameter estimates while Table 4-7 provides a summary of the results for each equation. Turning first to Table 4-6 and the parameter estimates, note that 11 of the 19 parameters are significant at the 5% level. All the demand elasticities have the correct sign and only the Spanish demand elasticity is insignificant. The differences in the size of the demand elasticities supports the hypothesis that carbon steel plate is differentiated. Notice that the U.S. demand elasticity is smaller than all of the foreign demand elasticities. This is what we would expect given the arguments of Jondrow, Chase and Gamble. The point estimate of the U.S. demand elasticity is small relative to Crandall's estimate of 1.81, but a 95% confidence interval is wide enough to allow for values as high as 1.93.

Turning to the technological parameters, note that while the scale parameter is highly significant, it is not significantly different from one at conventional levels. Thus the hypothesis of increasing returns can again be rejected. The remaining technological parameters are all insignificant, but this is due to multicollinearity. Using the procedure of Belsley et al mentioned above, multicollinearity was found to affect the standard errors of all of the input price coefficients.

Table 4-7 includes summary statistics for the individual equations. Again, the fits for the equations involving U.S. prices and output are good. The Brazilian and Canadian import demand equations also appear to fit well. The fits on the remaining import demand equations vary. Note that all the equations have been corrected for first order serial correlation.

Table 4-6: Parameter estimates for carbon steel plate

	Parameter estimate	Standard error	T-statistic
Constants			
$a_{bel,usa}$	-2.23	0.58	-3.93
$a_{bra,usa}$	34.78	5.32	6.53
$a_{can,usa}$	-2.17	0.57	-3.83
$a_{ger,usa}$	0.21	2.11	0.10
$a_{jap,usa}$	-4.17	1.86	-2.24
$a_{kor,usa}$	-2.34	2.14	-1.09
$a_{spa,usa}$	7.40	17.14	0.43
Demand elasticities			
$b_{bra} + 1$	10.83	1.27	8.51
$b_{can} + 1$	1.64	0.22	7.45
$b_{ger} + 1$	2.43	0.48	5.08
$b_{jap} + 1$	1.51	0.51	2.96
$b_{kor} + 1$	1.79	0.58	3.11
$b_{spa} + 1$	4.66	3.54	1.32
$b_{usa} + 1$	1.26	0.34	3.68
Technological parameters			
δ	1.08	0.06	19.51
ϕ_{labor}	19.36	32.57	0.59
ϕ_{bille}	179.43	228.00	0.79
ϕ_{energ}	-2.71	10.85	-0.25
ϕ_{capit}	-18.41	40.00	-0.46

Table 4-7: Equation results for carbon steel plate

Dependent variable	Mean	Root MSE	D.W. statistic
$\ln(X_{bel}/X_{usa})$	-3.22	0.52	2.20
$\ln(X_{bra}/X_{usa})$	-4.88	2.13	1.69
$\ln(X_{can}/X_{usa})$	-3.08	0.20	1.80
$\ln(X_{ger}/X_{usa})$	-4.25	0.58	2.24
$\ln(X_{jap}/X_{usa})$	-5.26	0.62	2.30
$\ln(X_{kor}/X_{usa})$	-3.90	0.73	2.26
$\ln(X_{spa}/X_{usa})$	-6.83	4.64	1.97
$\ln(X_{usa})$	12.81	0.14	1.89
$\ln(P_{usa})$	5.56	0.03	1.95

The results of the simulations for plate are given in Table 4-8. To simplify the exposition, I have combined the simulation results from the other six foreign countries into a single entity, the rest of the world (ROW). This is a misnomer in that there are many other foreign countries from which plate is imported which are not included in the study. The first two columns of Table 4-8 represent the effects of the antidumping duty levied against Brazil. In general, the effects of the antidumping duty on the domestic industry are small. U.S. output and profits rise by about four-tenths of one percent while U.S. prices decline by less than one-tenth on one percent. The antidumping duty raises imports from the ROW by about four-tenths of one percent, but the absolute increase in imports from the ROW is quite small when

Table 4-8: Simulation results for carbon steel plate

| Variable | Antidumping Duty | | Safeguard | |
	Absolute Change	% Change	Absolute Change	% Change
Imports and domestic output (in short tons)				
1. ROW Imports	1069	0.36	-13665	-4.69
2. Brazilian Imports	-26377	-99.72	-6796	-25.69
3. U.S. Output	7756	0.41	7756	0.41
4. Apparent Consumption	-17562	-0.80	-12706	-0.58
Prices, profits (both in 1984 dollars) and welfare				
5. U.S. Prices (average change)	-0.13	-0.07	-0.13	-0.07
6. U.S. Profits (in millions of dollars)	2.24	0.38	2.24	0.38
7. Welfare	-	-0.003	-	-0.09

compared with the absolute increase in U.S. output, so that trade diversion is weak. The antidumping duty has a prohibitive effect on Brazilian imports because the tariff is levied at an ad valorem rate of about 80%. Welfare again declines by a small amount, while apparent consumption falls by over three-fourths of one percent.

The size of the decline in apparent consumption is troubling because it indicates that the loss in Brazilian imports gives rise to only a small increase in the consumption of domestic output and other imports. How can this small increase be justified? One answer is that most of the Brazilian imports were diverted to countries not included in the study. Table 4-9 presents data on imports and the unit value of imports from different country groupings for 1983 and 1984. The foreign countries involved in the study (other than Brazil) are contained in the first group while Brazil itself forms the second group. The remaining Western European countries form the third group and the final group consists of all other countries. This group is dominated by Eastern European countries, South Africa, and Taiwan.

If Crandall's argument about the division of the U.S. steel market into two groups of buyers (those interested in security of supply and those interested in cost minimization) is correct, most of the trade diverted by the antidumping duty should have gone to producers whose plate has similar characteristics to Brazil's. As we can see in Table 4-9, Brazilian plate in 1983 was priced below all other varieties. The group most competitive with Brazil in terms of price was the ROW group, which contains Eastern Europe, South Africa, and Taiwan. If we combine this information with the assumption that all imports have roughly the same security of supply, it should be the case that most of trade diverted by the antidumping duty went to the ROW group.

But security of supply is not likely to be equal across imports. Imports from the developed countries (i.e. Japan, Korea, Canada, and Western Europe) are likely to have a much greater security of supply, primarily because their steel industries are well developed and have been exporting for a long time. Imports from Brazil and the Eastern European countries are likely to be much more volatile because their steel sectors do not have the same degree of stability. Thus imports from Brazil and some of the

Table 4-9: Unit values and import shares for carbon steel plate

		1983		1984	
		Unit value	Import share	Unit value	Import share
Group					
1.	Study group	288.83	54.44%	327.98	45.20%
2.	Brazil	273.59	18.47%	-	3.42%
3.	Other Western Europe	312.25	18.50%	341.56	17.73%
4.	ROW	284.24	8.59%	286.39	33.65%

Source: *U.S. General Imports: Schedule A.*

Group 1 - Belgium, Canada, West Germany, Japan, Korea, and Spain

Group 3 - Austria, Finland, France, Italy, Netherlands, Sweden, and United Kingdom

Group 4 - All others

countries in the ROW group should be close substitutes because they are also similar in terms of security of supply. Again, this implies that most of the diverted trade arising from the antidumping duty should go to the ROW countries.

When we look at the data provided in Table 4-9 for 1984, this is indeed the case. Notice first the large decrease in Brazil's share of total imports and the large increase in the share of total imports for the ROW group. The increase in the import share of the ROW group can be attributed to both the antidumping duty and to the higher prices charged by the developed countries. It is interesting to note that the developed country prices rose by nearly 13% while their combined imports declined by roughly the same amount. Given the nearly constant ROW prices, this is another sign of the degree of product differentiation across imports. In a market with homogeneous products, we would expect a 13% increase in price to have a much more negative impact on import share.

The above evidence suggests that Brazilian plate is a poor substitute for both U.S. plate and plate imported from developed countries. I provide additional evidence for this view in Table 4-10. In this table, I give the seven import cross price elasticities computed for U.S. plate over the sample period. Note in particular how low the Brazilian cross price elasticity is, both in absolute and relative terms. This provides further evidence that Brazilian steel is a poor substitute for both U.S. steel and the other imported steel included in the model.

The second two columns of Table 4-8 give the simulation results for the equivalent non-discriminatory safeguard. The tariff associated with the safeguard averaged about 2.9%. Several comments are in order. First, the bulk of the reduction in trade now falls on imports from the other countries included in the study group, although imports from Brazil still decline by about 25%. Second, the reduction in apparent consumption falls by about a third relative to that under the antidumping duty. This strengthens the substitutability argument given above. Finally, the welfare loss under the safeguard is much greater than that under the antidumping duty.

How can the antidumping duty be less costly to consumers than the safeguard when it reduces total consumption by more than the safeguard? The answer is that the composition of the

Table 4-10: Estimated cross price elasticities

Elasticity	Mean	Standard deviation	Maximum	Minimum
$\epsilon_{us,bel}$	0.021	0.002	0.036	0.018
$\epsilon_{us,bra}$	0.001	0.003	0.022	0.000
$\epsilon_{us,can}$	0.023	0.002	0.030	0.018
$\epsilon_{us,ger}$	0.019	0.004	0.030	0.011
$\epsilon_{us,jap}$	0.003	0.0002	0.004	0.002
$\epsilon_{us,kor}$	0.014	0.002	0.018	0.011
$\epsilon_{us,spa}$	0.002	0.002	0.009	0.000

Here $\epsilon_{i,j}$ gives the percentage change in i's output for a one percent change in j's price.

reduction in imports is important. With differentiated products, a reduction in one country's imports need not have the same effect on domestic welfare as an identical reduction in imports from another country. In this case, the antidumping duty reduces Brazilian imports while the safeguard reduces imports from all countries. The results show that the contribution of the latter imports to consumer welfare is much greater than the contribution of the imports from Brazil.

4.7 Conclusion

The results from this chapter show that the antidumping duties considered here had very little favorable impact on the domestic industry. In both cases, the duties had minimal effects on U.S. output, profits, and prices. In the case involving carbon steel plate, most of the benefits generated by the antidumping duty went to countries whose plate was competitive with Brazil's in terms of price. In the case involving stainless steel sheet and strip, the small size of the antidumping duties (about 5%) is probably responsible for the weak impact on U.S. producers. In either case, the idea that antidumping duties are a vehicle for protectionism does not fare well.

The results from the sheet and strip case agree with the conventional wisdom that antidumping duties are a less effective way of providing protection than non-discriminatory safeguards. This is because antidumping duties are by their nature discriminatory so their application leads to trade diversion. This trade diversion undermines their effectiveness. As a result, antidumping duties produce a greater welfare loss for a given level of protection.

The second case considered in this chapter shows that the extent of product differentiation can be an important factor in determining the efficacy of antidumping duties. The existence of trade diversion alone is not enough to make an antidumping duty less effective than a non-discriminatory alternative. The nature of the products involved is also important. In this case, the non-discriminatory tariff was less effective because it was levied against imports whose contribution to consumer welfare was greater than the imports which were subjected to the antidumping duty.

NOTES

1. The preferences used in Chapter 4 are more general than those used in Chapter 3. Thus the theoretical results of Chapter 3 will not necessarily apply. The main difference between the two sets of preferences is that those in Chapter 4 allow for an arbitrary pattern of substitutability between different varieties. The preferences in Chapter 3 are of the CES type.

2. See Helpman and Krugman for a proof.

3. The interpretation of δ as a scale parameter is valid only if capacity is not fully utilized.

4. The estimated equation is given by

$$UV_t = 26.56 - 71.68 \, D_1 + 1.08 \, HP_t - 0.74 \, HP_{t-1} -$$
$$ (0.4) \quad (-4.6) \qquad (3.1) \qquad (-1.8)$$

$$0.37 HP_{t-2} + 0.8 \, HP_{t-3} \quad R^2 = 0.75 \quad DW = 2.20$$
$$(-0.9) \qquad (2.3)$$

where t-statistics are given in parenthesis. UV represents the Spanish unit value index while HP represents the Spanish home price. D_1 is a dummy variable which takes the value of one after January of 1983, the period in which a countervailing duty was levied against Spanish exports of plate. The estimates have been corrected for first order serial correlation.

Conclusion

The most important premise of this study is that antidumping laws exist to provide relief to import competing industries. In the first part of this study, I show that the U.S. antidumping laws have been used successfully by domestic industries over the last decade to create a barrage of trade impediments. Of the 516 cases completed between 1980 and 1991, about 37% resulted in the imposition of antidumping duties. The average duty in these cases was 38%, which is large in comparison to most other tariffs or tariff equivalents. In addition to antidumping duties, the U.S. antidumping laws have also produced provisional protection in two out of three cases. Virtually all cases that made it past the preliminary ITC decision and were not withdrawn produced provisional protection. Finally, more than 20% of all antidumping cases were withdrawn prematurely. Most of these cases were withdrawn as a result of negotiated settlements; these settlements typically resulted in the imposition of VRAs.

Thus the U.S. antidumping laws have been used successfully to create trade barriers. But how effective have these barriers been in restricting imports and generating relief for U.S. industries? The two case studies in Chapter 4 suggest that the amount of relief generated by antidumping duties is not as great as the volume of trade barriers might suggest. In both of the case studies, imports did decline, but the presence of trade diversion and the fact that imports were differentiated from the domestic product prevented the decline in imports from being translated into significant gains for domestic producers. The results of two case studies do not imply that all antidumping duties are ineffective. But they do demonstrate that the protection provided by antidumping duties can be quite limited.

If the U.S. antidumping laws offer only limited protection, why have they been so widely used? One explanation is that the antidumping laws have become in large part a substitute for the escape clause. This is because the procedures used to determine the presence of dumping are tilted in favor of domestic producers. Since dumping is almost always found, the key question in most antidumping cases is whether the domestic industry is suffering material injury. Because the standards for material injury are weaker in antidumping cases than they are for escape clause cases, protection is more likely to be obatined (even if it is limited) through the antidumping laws.   Thus antidumping cases are a more attractive alternative for domestic producers.

Another explanation for the widespread use of the U.S. antidumping laws is that use of these laws has been implicitly encouraged. Evidence for this view is found in the failure of most escape clause actions. These actions have often been rejected because the trade involved was fair and because penalizing these imports would most likely have triggered some form of retaliation by foreign governments. As I show in Chapter 3, when foreign governments do retaliate, national welfare is often lower than it would be if the same amount of protection were provided through an antidumping duty. Thus antidumping duties are more attractive both because the political basis for them (unfair trade) is easier to rationalize and because there is no threat of overt retaliation when they are imposed. Antidumping duties are also more attractive from a political standpoint because they are discriminatory, something which is not true of escape clause actions. Discriminatory use of antidumping law allows domestic industries to focus their attention on the imports which are doing the most damage. Because antidumping cases usually involve only the most damaging imports, it is more difficult for countries to mount resistance to them. This is not true in escape clause cases where all imports are threatened. In these cases, the political resistance is greater because more countries are involved.

The arguments that I make above to explain the increased use of antidumping duties despite their apparent ineffectiveness have also been made by Bhagwati in the context of voluntary restraints agreements. VRAs share some of the key characteristics of antidumping duties and in many cases are the end result of antidumping cases. I quote from Bhagwati [1988].

> If a country's executive branch is characterized by the pro-trade bias I sketched above whereas its legislators must respond to protectionist pressure from various constituency groups, then it can be argued that a smart executive branch will prefer to use a porous form of protection that, while ensuring freer market access, will nonetheless appear to be a concession to political demands for protection from the legislators or from their constituencies. [pg. 58]

While the U.S. antidumping laws do not allow the executive branch to choose the degree of protection, it is certainly true that their use is politically appealing and satisfies demands for fair trade. It is also true that by discouraging the use of alternatives such as the escape clause, the executive office can effectively channel many trade complaints into the antidumping pipeline. Antidumping protection is also more porous than non-discriminatory alternatives and thus less likely to create trade disputes. All of these factors serve to explain why antidumping duties have become an increasingly important component of international trade policy.

Appendices

Appendix A

As stated in Chapter 2, the data used for the analysis of ITC decisions were drawn entirely from the final antidumping and countervailing duty reports of the ITC. In what follows, I briefly describe the data and some of the problems associated it. Before I discuss the variables themselves, I provide some background on the commissioners who served on the ITC during the sample period.

During the period under investigation (March, 1985 through December, 1990), 8 different commissioners served on the ITC. Two of the commissioners (Lodwick and Rohr) served on the commission over the entire period. Three commissioners (Stern, Liebeler and Eckes) began the period on the commission but eventually left. Commissioner Stern left in February of 1987, Commissioner Liebeler left in December of 1988, and Commissioner Eckes left in June of 1990. During the observation period, three new commissioners (Brunsdale, Cass and Newquist) were appointed. Commissioner Brunsdale was appointed in January, 1986, Commissioner Cass was appointed in January, 1988, and Commissioner Newquist was appointed in October, 1988. Commissioner Cass resigned in June of 1990.

Commissioners Eckes, Lodwick, Newquist, and Rohr consistently rendered bifurcated opinions while Commissioners Stern and Cass consistently rendered unified opinions. Commissioners Liebeler and Brunsdale switched their approach from bifurcated to unified in May, 1988. I have been unable to determine the reasons for this switch, but the addition of Commissioner Cass to the ITC in January of 1988 probably played an important role.

124 The Efficacy of Antidumping Duties

The dependent variables were taken from the opinions of the commissioners, which are included in the final report. The dependent variables represent the votes of the commissioners on issues pertaining only to actual material injury caused by the dumped or subsidized imports and not to any threat of material injury or to any material retardation resulting from the imports. While considerable care was exercised in collecting the votes, some ambiguities did arise and these should be mentioned. In a number of cases, commissioners offered bifurcated opinions in which they ruled negatively on both material injury and causation. These rulings at first blush appear to be inconsistent with bifurcation because the absence of material injury to the domestic industry makes any ruling on causation unnecessary. This inconsistency is cleared up by noting that the causation arguments are included for the sake of argument or for the sake of completeness. The commissioners themselves state repeatedly that the causation arguments are offered "assuming *arguendo*" that the domestic industry is materially injured. It should also be noted that in some cases, commissioners who normally used bifurcation were unable to come to any conclusion concerning the status of the domestic industry. In these cases, their opinions have been treated as unified.

Finally, it is not necessarily true that each commissioner cast only one vote (or one sequence of votes under bifurcation) in each case or that each commissioner casts the same number of votes in each case. In cases in which a commissioner finds more than one like product, that commissioner must vote on each of the like products. As an example, consider Certain Fresh Cut Flowers from Columbia. In that case, Commissioners Eckes, Lodwick and Rohr found that there were seven like products, and thus each cast seven votes, one for each like product. Commissioners Brunsdale and Liebeler found only one like product and thus voted only once on this product.

Consider next the independent variables. Domestic profit rates were obtained by taking the ratio of operating income to net sales. Both domestic and foreign market share data are based on the volume of shipments wherever possible. When data on the volume of shipments was not available, market shares were based on the value of shipments. Domestic employment levels reflect the number of workers involved in the production of the product under investigation while domestic production reflects the volume of output of the product under investigation. Data on domestic shipments, unfair imports, and apparent consumption were expressed, wherever possible, in terms of volumes. When the volume data was not available, values were used instead. Unit values for domestic shipments were obtained by dividing the value of domestic shipments by the volume of these shipments. The dumping and subsidy margins were taken directly from the reports. It should be noted that in several cases, a specific rather than ad valorem margin was given. These cases were dropped from the data set.

The market share of dumped or subsidized imports (FMS) was adjusted to allow for the cumulation of imports. Cumulation takes place in cases involving dumped or subsidized imports from more than one country. In these cases, if the imports are sufficiently similar, the ITC must cumulatively assess the impact of the dumped imports on the domestic industry. This means that for the purposes of addressing causation, the import shares must be combined across some or all of the countries involved in the investigation.

Appendix B

In this appendix, I prove two results which are used frequently in Chapter 3.

Result 1: $\phi_{31} \phi_{22} - \phi_{21} \phi_{32} > 0$

Proof: Substituting for the ϕ's and manipulating, Result 1 requires that

$$(P_{31} X_{31} / P_{21} X_{21}) - (P_{32} X_{32} / P_{22} X_{22}) > 0$$

This expression can be reduced to

$$(c_2 / c_3)^{b_1 - b_2} - 1 > 0$$

Since we have assumed that $c_2 > c_3$ and that $b_1 > b_2$, this condition will hold.

■

Result 2: $\sigma_{22} \sigma_{31} - \sigma_{21} \sigma_{32} > 0$

Proof: Substituting for the σ's and manipulating, Result 2 requires that

$$(X_{22} X_{31} / X_{21} X_{32}) - 1 > 0$$

This condition reduces to

$$(c_2 / c_3)^{b_1 - b_2} - 1 > 0$$

From the proof for Result 1, we know that this condition holds.

■

Appendix C

In this appendix, I prove two propositions discussed in Chapter 3.

Proposition 1: *The number of product varieties produced worldwide increases after the imposition of an antidumping duty.*

Proof: The expression for the change in the number of product varieties produced worldwide is given by

$$N_{ad} = \sum_{i=1}^{3} \epsilon_i N_{iad}$$

where $\epsilon_i = N_i / N$ and N_{ad} is the change in the number of varieties produced worldwide after the antidumping duty is imposed. Since N_{1ad} is positive, N_{ad} will be positive if

$$\epsilon_2 N_{2ad} + \epsilon_3 N_{3ad} > 0$$

Substituting and manipulating the left hand side of this equation, we find that this equation will hold if

$$N_2 \phi_{32} - N_3 \phi_{22} > 0$$

This condition can be reduced to

$$(c_2 / c_3)^{b_2} - 1 > 0$$

This condition holds because we have assumed that $c_2 > c_3$.

■

Proposition 2: *The number of product varieties produced worldwide increases after the imposition of a non-discriminatory tariff.*

Proof: The expression for the change in the number of varieties produced worldwide is given by

$$N_{sg} = \sum_{i=1}^{3} \epsilon_i N_{isg}$$

where N_{sg} is the change in the number of varieties produced worldwide after the imposition of the safeguard. We must show that this expression is positive. Substituting and manipulating, we must show that

$$D_{3sg} \left[(N_3 \phi_{22} - N_2 \phi_{32}) \phi_{11} + N_1 (\phi_{32} \phi_{21} - \phi_{22} \phi_{31}) \right]$$

$$+ N_1 (1 - \phi_{11}) b_1 t_{sg} + D_{2sg} (N_2 \phi_{11} - N_1 \phi_{21}) > 0$$

Since D_{2sg}, D_{3sg}, and $(\phi_{32} \phi_{21} - \phi_{22} \phi_{31})$ are all negative, the entire expression will be positive if

(1) $N_3 \phi_{22} - N_2 \phi_{32} < 0$

(2) $N_2 \phi_{11} - N_1 \phi_{21} < 0$

Condition (1) was proved in Proposition 1. Condition (2) reduces, after some manipulation, to

$$(c_1 / c_2)^{b_1} - 1 > 0$$

This condition holds because we have assumed that $c_1 > c_2$.

■

Appendix D

In this appendix, I demonstrate the conditions under which equation (3.32) is non-negative. This equation will be non-negative if and only if

$$(\sigma_{22} \sigma_{31} - \sigma_{21} \sigma_{32}) b_3 - \sigma_{21} \sigma_{33} b_2 \geq 0$$

Substituting for the σ's and simplifying, this condition can be rewritten as

$$(D.1) \quad (c_2/c_3)^{b_1 - b_2} - 1 \geq \frac{l_3 - e_3}{l_2 - e_2} \frac{b_2 + 1}{b_3 + 1} [\frac{N_2}{N_3} (c_2/c_3)^{-b_2} + 1]$$

To simplify further, we need to derive expressions for the initial values of N_2 and N_3. There are two cases to be considered: the case in which ϕ_{32} does not equal zero and the case in which ϕ_{32} equals zero.

Case 1: ϕ_{32} not equal to zero.

In this case, I will show that (2.32) must be negative. Combining the demand equations, the first order conditions and the zero profit conditions and solving, I find that

$$N_2 = \frac{l_2 - e_2}{[F_2 - F_1 (c_1/c_2)^{b_1}] [b_2 + 1]} - (c_2/c_3)^{b_2} N_3$$

$$N_3 = \frac{(l_3-e_3)/(b_3+1)}{F_3 - F_1(c_1/c_3)^{b_1} - [F_2 - F_1(c_1/c_2)](c_2/c_3)^{b_2}}$$

Substituting these definitions into (D.1) yields

$$(D.2) \quad \frac{F_2}{F_3} \geq (c_2/c_3)^{-b_1}$$

This is a necessary and sufficient condition which insures that (2.32) is non-negative. I now demonstrate that when this condition holds, one country produces a negative number of product varieties in the initial equilibrium. This means that (D.2) will not hold in any equilibrium so that (2.32) must be negative. To see this, note that necessary conditions for both N_2 and N_3 to be positive and bounded are

$$(i) \quad F_2 - F_1 (c_1/c_2)^{b_1} > 0$$

$$(ii) \quad F_3 - F_2 (c_2/c_3)^{b_2} + F_1 (c_1/c_2)^{b_1} [(c_2/c_3)^{b_2} - (c_2/c_3)^{b_1}] > 0$$

Condition (ii) is less likely to hold as F_2 becomes larger. Let F_2^* denote the value of F_2 such that (i) holds with equality. For $F_2 \leq F_2^*$, N_2 is unbounded. But it is also true that if (ii) does not hold at F_2^*, it will not hold for F_2 greater than F_2^*. Now substitute out F_1 in condition (ii) using the definition of F_2^*. Then (ii) will be positive (and N_3 will be positive and bounded) only if

$$\frac{F_2^*}{F_3} < (c_2/c_3)^{-b_1}$$

This condition contradicts (D.2), and hence (2.32) must be negative when ϕ_{32} is not equal to zero.

Case 2: ϕ_{32} equal to 0.

In this case, I will show that (2.32) may be positive. Solving for N_2 and N_3, we now find that

$$N_2 = \frac{I_2 - e_2}{[F_2 - F_1 \, (c_1 / c_2)^{b_1}] \, [b_2 + 1]}$$

$$N_3 = \frac{I_3 - e_3}{[F_3 - F_1 \, (c_1 / c_3)^{b_1}] \, [b_3 + 1]}$$

Substituting these definitions of N_2 and N_3 into (D.1), we find that (2.32) will be non-negative if and only if (D.2) holds. Necessary and sufficient conditions for both N_2 and N_3 to be positive and bounded are

(i) $\quad F_2 - F_1 \, (c_1 / c_2)^{b_1} > 0$

(ii) $\quad F_3 - F_1 \, (c_1 / c_3)^{b_1} > 0$

These conditions do not place any upper bound on F_2 and hence they do not contradict (D.2). Thus (2.32) may be positive when $\phi_{32} = 0$.

References

Amemiya, Takeshi. 1985. *Advanced Econometrics*. Cambridge: Harvard University.

Armington, Paul S. 1969. "A Theory of Demand for Products Distinguished by Place of Production." *IMF Staff Papers 16*, 159-78.

Baldwin, Robert E. 1985. *The Political Economy of U.S. Import Policy*. Cambridge: The MIT Press.

Baldwin, Robert E., and Michael O. Moore. 1991. "Administration of the Trade Remedy Laws by the Department of Commerce: A Political Economy Analysis." In *Down in the Dumps: Administration of the Unfair Trade Laws*, edited by Richard Boltuck and Robert Litan, 245-280. Washington: The Brookings Institute.

Baldwin, Robert E., and Jeffrey W. Steagall. 1991. "An Analysis of Factors Influencing ITC Decisions in Antidumping, Countervailing Duty, and Safeguards Cases." Paper presented at the University of Wisconsin - Free University of Brussels Conference on "Are the Fair Trade and Safeguards Laws Operating as Intended?" Washington, D.C.

Belsley, D.A., E. Kuh, and R.E. Welsch. 1980. *Regression Diagnostics, Identifying Influential Data and Sources of Collinearity*. New York: Wiley.

Bhagwati, Jagdish. 1988. *Protectionism*. Cambridge: The MIT Press.

133

Brander, James, and Paul Krugman. 1983. "A Reciprocal Dumping Model of International Trade." *Journal of International Economics 15*, 313-21.

Bryan, Greyson. 1980. *Taxing Unfair International Trade Practices: A Study of U.S. Antidumping and Countervailing Duty Laws.* Lexington: Heath, 1980.

Caine, Wesley K. 1981. "A Case for Repealing the Antidumping Provisions of the Tariff Act of 1930." *Law and Policy in International Business 13*, 681-726.

Crandall, Robert W. 1981. *The U.S. Steel Industry in Recurrent Crisis: Policy Options in a Competitive World.* Washington: The Brookings Institute.

Destler, I.M. 1986. *American Trade Politics: System Under Stress.* Washington: Institute for International Economics.

Dixit, A.K., and J.E. Stiglitz. 1977. "Monopolistic Competition and Optimum Product Diversity." *American Economic Review 67*, 297-308.

Duke, Richard M., Richard L. Johnson, Hans Mueller, P. David Qualls, Calvin T. Rush Jr. and David G. Tarr. 1977. *The United States Steel Industry and Its International Rivals.* Staff Report of the Bureau of Economics.

Eichengreen, Barry, and Hans Van der Ven. 1984. "U.S. Antidumping Policies: The Case of Steel." in *The Structure and Evolution of Recent U.S. Trade Policy*, edited by R.E. Baldwin and A. Krueger, 68-103. Chicago: University of Chicago Press.

Either, Wilfred J. 1982. "Dumping." *Journal of Political Economy 90*, 487-506.

Finger, J. Michael, and Tracy Murray. 1990. "Policing Unfair Imports: The United States Example." *Journal of World Trade 24*, 39-53.

Flam, Harry, and Elhanan Helpman. 1987. "Industrial Policy under Monopolistic Competition." *Journal of International Economics 22*, 79-102.

Gallant, A.R., and D.W. Jorgenson. 1979. "Statistical Inference for a System of Simultaneous, Nonlinear, Implicit Equations in the Context of Instrumental Variables Estimation." *Journal of Econometrics 11,* 275-302.

Grossman, Gene M. 1986. "Imports as a Cause of Injury: The Case of the Steel Industry." *Journal of International Economics 20*, 201-23.

Gruenspecht, Howard K. 1987. "Dumping and Dynamic Competition." Working Paper, Carnegie Mellon University.

Hansen, Wendy L. 1990. "The ITC and the Politics of Protection." *American Political Science Review 84*, 21-45.

Hearn, Anthony C., and Larry R. Seward. 1987. *Reduce User's Guide for the DEC Vax 11: Version 3.2*. Santa Monica: The Rand Corporation.

Helpman, Elhanan. 1984. "Increasing Returns, Imperfect Markets and Trade Theory." in *Handbook of International Economics*, edited by R.W. Jones and P.B. Kenen, 325-365. New York: North-Holland.

Helpman, E., and P. Krugman. 1985. *Market Structure and Foreign Trade*. Cambridge: The MIT Press.

Herander, Mark G., and J. Brad Schwartz. 1984. "An Empirical Test of the Threat of U.S. Trade Policy: The Case of Antidumping Duties." *Southern Economic Journal 51*, 59-79.

Hindley, Brian. 1990. "The Economics of Dumping and Anti-Dumping Action: Is there a Baby in the Bathwater?" in *Policy Implications of Antidumping Measures*, edited by P.K.M. Tharakan, 25-43. New York: North Holland.

Hoekman, Bernard M., and Michael P. Leidy. 1989. "Dumping, Antidumping and Emergency Protection." Working Paper.

Howell, Thomas R., William A. Noellert, Jesse G. Kreier, and Alan W. Wolff. 1988. *Steel and the State*. Boulder: Westview Press.

Jondrow, James, David Chase, and Christopher Gamble. 1982. "The Price Differential between Domestic and Imported Steel." *Journal of Business 55*, 383-399.

Jones, Kent. 1986. *Politics vs. Economics in World Steel Trade*. London: Allen and Unwin.

Kaplan, Seth. 1991. "Injury and Causation in USITC Antidumping Determinations: Five Recent Approaches." in *Policy Implications of Antidumping Measures*, edited by P.K.M. Tharakan, 143-173. New York: North Holland.

Lancaster, Kelvin. 1984. "Protection and Product Differentiation." in *Monopolistic Competition and International Trade*, edited by H. Kierzkowski, 137-156. Oxford: Clarendon Press.

Levine, Michael K. 1985. *Inside International Trade Policy Formulation*. New York: Praeger Publishers.

Maddala, G. S. 1983. *Limited Dependent and Qualitative Variables in Econometrics*. Cambridge: Cambridge University Press.

Messerlin, Patrick A. 1989. "The EC Antidumping Regulations: A First Economic Appraisal, 1980-85." *Weltwirtschaftliches Archiv 125*, 563-587.

Moore, Michael O. 1988. *U.S. Antidumping Procedures as a Repeated Game: A Theoretical and Empirical Analysis*. Ph.D. Dissertation. University of Wisconsin.

Moore, Michael O. 1990. "Rules or Politics?: An Empirical Analysis of ITC Antidumping Decisions." Economics Discussion Paper D-9005. George Washington University.

Morkre, Morris E., and Harold E. Kruth. 1989. "Determining Whether Dumped or Subsidized Imports Injure Domestic Industries: ITC Approach." *Contemporary Policy Issues 7*, 78-95.

Murray, Tracy. 1991. "The Administration of the Antidumping Duty Law by the Department of Commerce." In *Down in the Dumps: Administration of the Unfair Trade Laws*, edited by Richard Boltuck and Robert Litan, 23-63. Washington: The Brookings Institute.

Norall, Christopher. 1986. "New Trends in Antidumping Law in Brussels." *The World Economy 9*, 97-111.

Palmeter, David N. 1983. "Countervailing Subsidized Imports: The ITC Goes Astray." *Pacific Basin Law Journal 1*, 1-34.

Palmeter, David N. 1987a. "Injury Determinations in Antidumping and Countervailing Duty Cases - A Commentary on U.S. Practice." *Journal of World Trade Law 2*, 123-161.

Palmeter, David N. 1987b. "Dumping Margins and Material Injury: The USITC is Free to Choose." *Journal of World Trade Law 4*, 173-5.

Prusa, Thomas J. 1988. *International Trade Policies, Incentives, and Firm Behavior*. Ph.D. Dissertation. Stanford University.

Prusa, Thomas J. 1990. "The Selection of Antidumping Cases for ITC Determination." Paper delivered at the Conference on Empirical Studies of Commercial Policy, Cambridge, MA.

Staiger, Robert W., and Frank A. Wolak. 1989. "Strategic Use of Antidumping Law to Enforce Tacit International Collusion." NBER Working Paper #3016.

Stegemann, Klaus. 1991. "The International Regulation of Dumping: Protection Made Too Easy." *The World Economy 14*, 375-405.

Tarr, David G. 1979. "Cyclical Dumping." *Journal of International Economics 9*, 57-63.

UNCTAD. 1984. *Protectionism and Structural Assistance: Antidumping and Countervailing Duty Practices*.

United States International Trade Commission. *Annual Report*. Various Years.

United States International Trade Commission. *Operation of the Trade Agreements Program*. Various Years.

United States International Trade Commission. 1984. *Special and Administrative Provisions: Titles III, IV and VII of the Tariff Act of 1930 and Related Laws*. Publication #1760.

Varian, Hal R. 1978. *Microeconomic Analysis*. New York: W.W. Norton and Company.

Webb, Michael J. 1987. "Antidumping Laws, Production Location, and Prices." *Journal of International Economics 22*, 363-8.

Yarrow, George. 1987. "Economic Aspects of Antidumping Policies." *Oxford Review of Economic Policy 3*, 66-79.

Index